MW01281983

THE GOD MAKERS

Dr. Richard C. Cheatham

authorHOUSE®

AuthorHouse™
1663 Liberty Drive
Bloomington, IN 47403
www.authorhouse.com
Phone: 1-800-839-8640

First published by AuthorHouse 7/8/2009

ISBN: 978-1-4389-9393-5 (sc)

Library of Congress Control Number: 2009905705

The Author combines an encounter with a "poltergeist" with his
own spiritual journey to weave a tale of mind and mystery which
challenges traditional Church theology and authority.

Printed in the United States of America
Bloomington, Indiana

This book is printed on acid-free paper.

PROLOGUE

I suppose I wrote this tale more for myself than for the reader. It is something I needed to write – to clarify my own understanding of a few events and changes in my life. I never planned to become a Christian clergyman. In fact, when I learned that a former schoolmate of mine was entering the ministry I openly wondered why he would throw his life away like that. I was happily engaged in the family boat and sporting goods business. My plans were to eventually sell our starter house, move back to Grosse Pointe, join a club, and live the good life.

God, however, had other plans for me.

A powerful, mystical call sent me scurrying for a preacher's license so I could support my family by serving a church while earning the academic credentials I needed for full ordination as a Methodist minister. Somewhere in that process I focused so completely upon the academics that I lost my spiritual perspective. It was in the small village of Napoleon, Michigan, where I served a student charge that I had an extraordinary experience which began to put me back on track. The Christian faith is not just an intellectual structure to be understood and believed. It is a spiritual journey to be lived.

Many years later, as I struggled to more fully understand this experience and my ensuing journey, I conceived the idea of using the motif of the carpool. Every week, for four years, I rode two hundred and fifty miles to and from Evanston, Illinois to attend Garrett Theological Seminary. I used – and created – the conversations en route to show my personal transition and to present the spiritual/intellectual journey that accompanied – and continued beyond it.

The carpool is more than a literary device, however. It actually follows the general tone and flow of the conversations and relationships that were formed. Because the composition of the group varied over time, some characters are composites – some are not. They all represent people for whom I still feel deep affection. Some of the dialogues were drawn from remembrances of actual conversations. However, all of the dialogues dealing with the title are of my construction.

The episodes dealing with my family are true to life.

The many incidents at a parishioner's house occurred precisely as I report them. Although they happened more than forty years ago, they were unforgettable. The reader will soon discover why that is so.

As I wrote the account, I realized it might be of value for others to read. Thus the tale became a book. I invite you to join me in reliving this adventure of a lifetime.

ACKNOWLEDGEMENTS

As with my first book, *Can You Make the Buttons Even?*, I owe so many for the understandings I share: Questions posed; observations made; information offered – in and out of classrooms; encounters with strangers; rich adventures of the spirit, encountered in a variety of ways.

Some friends read the early drafts and gave their comments and suggestions. I thank them for their advice and words of encouragement. I am particularly grateful to Debbie Guidry, whose extensive editorial insights and comments helped me to rethink, refocus and sharpen the final draft.

I want to acknowledge the aid of my friend and fellow author, Dr. David Roberts for his specific insights and observations. I also need to thank Margaret and Amy Valade for their insightful critiques which helped to give the book its final shape.

The loving encouragement and support of Diane, my patient, proofreading wife, is an important portion of every accomplishment attributed to me.

All these have joined to create the understandings I attempt to share in this little tale.

CHAPTER 1

It had been another long and tedious drive home. Five and a half hours of a winding, hilly secondary highway that wended its way through every small town in Southwest Michigan. Four years of this to get the degree Dick needed to stay home and work full time at his church. Four years of getting up at six A.M. on Mondays, rushing to get himself dressed and fed, kissing the girls goodbye, and rushing to be ready for Leonard when he came by at 6:45. Four years of carpooling the two hundred and fifty miles to Evanston, Illinois. Diane, God bless her, always got up and fixed their breakfast. They would chat as they ate, trying to cram in the last bit of conversation they would be able to share until Friday evening. Then, always reluctantly, and always too hastily, they embraced and kissed, as Dick turned the doorknob and rushed out into the darkness.

Leonard was usually on time. He had been a farmer prior to entering the ministry, so he was accustomed to rising early. He and Dick would chat about their weekend ordeals as they headed westward, picking up the others on the way. Without realizing it Dick had come to recognize every landmark and unconsciously knew to the minute when they would see the next in line. They would stop for lunch along the route. Something quick: A hamburger and bowl of chili. Then they would see the skyline of Chicago about noon, and arrive in Evanston in time for the first class at 1:00. It was all so predictable. .

. . It was all so boringly predictable.

The ride, itself, was not so bad - yet. It was early autumn. The roads were mostly dry, and the darkness did not yet settle in on them so early. The trees were beginning to turn from green to various shades of reds and yellows, transforming the landscape into a glorious array of pastels, which - according to James Whitcomb Riley - created a "picture that no painter has the colorin' to mock." Dick smiled at the recollection of that long-ago memorized poem. *9th grade; Mrs. Pohlabel.* She had insisted that the class memorize a few selected poems. He had not understood why. It seemed a useless waste of time and brain storage space. He was to learn over the years, however, that this foolish busy work had taught him an appreciation for poetry, and caused him to memorize verses which came back from time to time to warm his heart or give some word of encouragement or understanding. He smiled to himself as he reflected upon the many now-forgotten teachers of his youth who had imparted some portion of their wisdom, hoping against hope that it might take root and bear fruit with the passing of the years. Now, he had moved into the position of being the one who passed along some of the wisdom of the ages. *A dispenser of wisdom and encouragement on weekends and a student from Monday through Friday.* Again, he smiled to himself as he considered the irony of his situation.

Dick looked about at the others in the carpool. They helped pass the time as they shared sermon ideas, debated everything from theology to politics, and filled the remaining conversational time with family news, sports and entertainment. As with any group brought together by necessity, some were interesting and entertaining and some were not. Fortunately, Dick reflected, the latter was the last on and first off.

Everyone was eager to get home. Yet everyone knew the short weekend would be hectic, filled with meetings, hospital calls, counseling sessions, sermon preparation and worship services. It was difficult to plan for adequate time with the family. Unless there was an emergency, Friday evening was dedicated to the family. Dick spent a short time with each daughter to catch up on her week. Then they had dinner in the kitchen (the parsonage had no dining room). He usually took the family to the hospital with him after church on Sunday. It was about twenty miles away in Jackson. They would talk and sing and play games while driving. If the weather permitted, the children played with Diane in the nearby park while Dick made the obligatory calls. Then they would all go out for Sunday dinner at a nice restaurant afterward. If there had been a wedding or funeral on Saturday, the meal would include a nice steak. It was the 60's and the typical ten dollar honorarium could make the difference between chicken and prime ribs.

Two and a half years of this routine. One and a half more to go. Dick took comfort in the thought that he was more than half way through and they were still functioning as a family. *Grace and hard work*, he thought to himself with a smile, as he entered the little parsonage that served as their family home. Diane stood grinning, as Deb rushed to greet him. Fourteen years, and Diane still was as lovely as when they first met. Her brown eyes glowed when she smiled and she was always able to lift his spirits or convey a coy invitation without speaking a word. Deb was all smiles and bubbles as Dick lifted her up to head level, squeezed her a hug and kissed her warmly. He always wanted to hold that moment a bit longer, but there were others who had to be greeted - and whom he wanted to hug warmly, as well. Next it was Diane's turn. They paused for a brief moment, almost like strangers as they measured themselves and felt the closeness return. Their days apart were lived so differently that a chasm always seemed to open up. It was a chasm that needed to be closed, and could be closed, but took a moment to measure and diminish. Then Diane and Dick embraced - always with just enough proper restraint for the benefit of Deb. Her age had hit double digits now and she was beginning to show an interest in such matters. Dick decided that he needed to ask Diane to have "that little talk" with her before long. Then he released Diane reluctantly, hoping that the late evening might find them able to avoid the restraint. Diane would nod toward the back study, and Dick walked there slowly, and peered into the unlighted room at Cindy, sitting silently in her small chair. This, too, was a part of the very predictable routine. Deb was eleven and seemed to take these Monday departures and Friday returns in stride. Cindy was just eight, and quietly . . . at some subterranean level . . . feared that her daddy just might not return this time. Every Friday evening, like clockwork, she would disappear into the darkness and sit silently waiting until Dick would come into the room, kneel down and gently take her into his arms. As with Diane, he could feel the distance between them melt away in the tenderness of an embrace. After a few minutes all was normal again. The evening meal was set and life at the Napoleon church parsonage was resumed.

The phone rang! "It's an official dinner!" the girls chimed. Dick headed for the phone, tacitly complaining as he went, W*hy can't the parishioners wait for me to have dinner with my family?*

"Pastor Dick?" a women's voice inquired.

"You're speaking to him," he responded. Dick was now becoming accustomed to that title, which had at first seemed so strange.

She identified herself as Irene Gerston. Dick remembered her. She was a quiet, person - not particularly active - more of a pew sitter than an active participant. Her husband rarely attended. *That could be part of the reason*, he thought, as he waited for her to continue.

"Do you know what a poltergeist is?" the voice inquired timidly.

"It's a mischievous spirit." Dick responded, vaguely remembering a dictionary definition he had read years ago. For a moment he wondered where the conversation was going. He hoped she had not interrupted their dinner just to help settle a family argument.

"What do you think about them?" she asked in such a manner that caused Dick to know there was something more than an intellectual debate at stake.

"I think they might be a genuine phenomenon," he answered, realizing that he had said nothing at all definitive, but hopefully enough to allow her to continue.

"Would you please come over?" she asked in a tone that was almost pleading. "I think we have one."

Dick hesitated for a moment, aware that the dinner was on the table. The family had been waiting a week for this time together. The few years in professional ministry had taught him that most emergencies can wait a spell. He decided to give it a try: "I have some things to take care of. Would an hour be soon enough?"

"Yes, yes, please. I'll see you in an hour."

Dick hung up the phone, and silently cursed to himself. The phone had been close enough to the kitchen so that he knew they had all heard the one way conversation, particularly the promise to be there (wherever *there* was) in an hour. *There goes our Friday evening.* Everyone knew it. Yet, Diane, Deb and Cindy were all good soldiers. They would not complain. This was the price they all paid for his deciding he had been called into the ministry. When he returned to the table the mood had sobered. "I have to go out."

"We heard," said Diane. No complaint, but with a tone of disappointment which spoke for everyone.

"I'll try to make it quick." Dick offered.

"That's okay, Daddy," Deb said, trying to regain her smile. "We'll see you later." Cindy just sat quietly, playing with her food. Something within Dick withered. The food - once delightful and savory - had lost its appeal. A part of him wished he were still back in the business of selling boats. The springs and summers were always late nights, but when he did get home, he stayed home. *I just wish . . .* The thought trailed off into nowhere, as Dick sat awkwardly finishing the meal, trying to pick up the light-hearted conversation which also had trailed off into nowhere.

After dinner, he drove to Irene's. It was about a half a mile away, on one of the newer streets in the tiny, old village. In retrospect, he thought he must have driven through Alice's looking glass on the way. From that moment until the end of the episode, nothing made sense. Yet *everything* made sense.

Dick drove slowly down the street, trying to see the house numbers through the darkness. Finally he arrived at what appeared to be the right number, pulled the car up, and started to get out. Then he froze! A deep-throated, threatening roar erupted from the darkness. He quickly closed the door. *Okay, guy, what are you going to do?* Dick asked himself. There obviously was a rather large, dog out there who was telling him that he was not welcome. *The question*, he thought*, is whether or not someone had the good sense to keep you caged or chained.* He sat quietly for a minute, feeling awkward, but not quite ready to trust himself to the benevolence of whatever that was out there telling him he was not welcome. Then the porch light turned on, and the front door opened.

"Pastor Dick?" Irene stepped into the light. "Don't worry about Major. He's just telling me I have a visitor." With that assurance Dick emerged awkwardly from the car and walked hastily to the house. He kept watching for Major, but could not see him. He tried listening to ascertain where he was, just in case Major decided Irene needed additional warning or protection. But there was not another sound. It was hard to maintain some sense of dignity while his head swung back and forth like a pendulum and his body assumed a crouched position ready to ward off any attack. *This was something they never taught at seminary: Dog Defense 101*, he thought. *I may suggest it to the dean.*

"You never have to worry about Major when he's barking," Irene explained.

"It's when he's silent that he's stalking you." Dick filed that away, and from that time on he always waited until he heard the barking before he unlocked his car door.

Irene did not bother with niceties, for which Dick was pleased. There usually was an offer of tea or coffee; maybe some pastries or mints before people got around to talking. Early into this venture of ministry he had realized that an occupational hazard well may be coffee nerves or gout. Irene jumped right into the issue without even offering a chair.

"Some strange things have been happening, and I need to fill you in from back at the beginning." Without hesitation, she continued: "We used to live in a trailer, about two miles out of town, off of highway 52."

Dick nodded. "I know the place." It was a shabby area, no street lights, a junk yard not too far away. Rows of trees hid the fields and most of the junk yard. The road into the trailer park was unpaved. Mostly dirt, some gravel.

Irene continued. "It was lonely out there, and Danny had an imaginary playmate, or at least I thought so at the time. He would talk with her and tell me about her. She was an older woman." I knew Danny was her young son, about five years old now. Diane had taught him at Head Start a year or so ago. Dick just nodded. There was no need to interrupt with questions or comments. Irene was going to tell her story: Her *entire* story.

"It usually happened when I was pregnant." She hastily explained. "I've had many miscarriages. Walter was hardly ever around. He spends most evenings with his men friends." Dick pictured Walter: a classic redneck if ever there was one. They never looked like they went together. He looked like a typical high school dropout who spent his spare time hunting, fishing, drinking beer and bowling, while Irene presented herself as someone who could have - and should have - done much better. She appeared somewhat ordinary: average height, nice average appearing face, but her eyes carried a sense of intelligence and she had a pleasant smile. *Young love! Dick* thought. *There's no accounting for what it does to people.* Irene was still talking so he quickly refocused upon what she was trying to explain to him.

"It's hard to explain, but there just seemed to be something strange happening in that trailer." She paused and looked at Dick carefully, as though to appraise how he was receiving this vague information. Dick tried to appear sensitive and sympathetic, but his mind was racing to explain Irene's assumption that a poltergeist was somehow involved in her life. *Alone and pregnant - with an imaginative little son. It wouldn't take too much to push her into letting her imagination run wild.* He was already beginning to write off whatever it was that had upset Irene enough for her to call him.

Irene seemed to sense that she had best leave out vague events and jump to the specific details. "We moved here recently, and I had the space to put up all my pictures and family photos." She pointed to a knick knack shelf filled with small, family photos. "I brought out the photograph of my mother and set it here. When Danny saw it he said, 'That's the lady I've been talking to, Mommy.' I couldn't believe it," she said. "My mother died before Danny was born. He never saw her or her picture." This hit Dick unexpectedly and he felt a chill pass through him, but only for a moment. He reasoned *A lot of old women look alike to little kids. The clothing might have done it.* Dick thought that, but said nothing, letting Irene continue her tale. There obviously had to be something more. So far she was hinting at a ghost. A poltergeist had to be doing something more than talk with her son. Dick believed that neither was likely, but his curiosity was whetted.

"That evening, Walter came home and saw my mother's picture. 'What's that doing here?' he yelled. 'You know I don't want pictures of dead people hanging around my house!' We argued, but Walter insisted, so I put mother's picture away." She paused, looked around as though she wanted to be certain no one else was listening. Then in a quiet, confidential tone, as though telling a secret, she said:

"The next morning all the pictures in the house had been knocked over . . . and some chairs had been tipped over, as well."

Okay, Dick thought, *what have we got here? Kinetic energy? Danny playing games? Could Irene be a sleep walker?* He said nothing. He merely nodded, waiting for Irene to continue. And she did.

"That was just the start of it." She led Dick into the living room, and pointed at the sofa. "Every evening, when I'm here alone, when Danny is in bed and there is only Minnie and I here -" she hastened to explain. "Minnie is our indoor dog." She pointed to a small, mongrel lying quietly (possibly sleeping) on the floor. "Minnie will suddenly sit up and act like she's watching someone. Her hair bristles and she stands very still - rigid, really - her back arches - and she just turns her

10

head slowly as though she sees someone moving across the room. And at the same time, I can hear footsteps and *feel* a presence. It's frightening!" She shuddered as she spoke those final words.

"How often does this happen?"

"Every night now."

Finally! This was something he could sink his teeth into! A nightly visitor. There had to be some logical explanation. *Find it. Ease this lady's fears. Go home.*

"What time does this usually occur?"

"Sometime after 11:00."

"I'll come back tonight just before 11:00. You will go to bed and leave me alone here in the living room. I'll find out what this is. Okay?"

She smiled a smile of relief. "Please . . . please do."

Dick went to the door. Opened it. Waited until he heard the barking, went directly to the car and drove home. As he drove, he reviewed the details of the brief meeting.

Damn! he thought. *Am I dealing with a neurotic, a nut, or What?*

He was soon to discover it was the *What.*

Chapter 2

"We waited to have dessert together." Diane greeted Dick as he came through the door.

"Great!" I was afraid you might have eaten it all up," he responded with a grin. It felt good to know that he was still enough of a part of the family that this just wasn't one more night without daddy. For a moment Dick felt a twinge of sadness for the single students at seminary. Maybe they did not miss their family all week as the married ones did. But they had no one to come home to, either. They had no one who wondered how they were, and who missed them when they were away. *It's a trade off,* Dick said to himself. *But I'll settle for what I've got over anything those single guys have.*

The girls giggled and ran for the kitchen table. They had wanted to be with their daddy but were also eager to get the pie and ice cream which Diane had picked out especially for tonight. Each girl snuggled up close to Dick's end of the table. He knew they missed him as much as he missed being with them and seeing them every day. This was a terrible price to pay, but it was something he knew he absolutely had to do. Dick had been successful in the business world, but was never satisfied. He had garnered some of the trophies of success. He had a growing collection of big boy toys, but most of them quickly lost their appeal. Then Dick had experienced this powerful, even mystical, call to become a preacher. Diane had hesitated. *Understandably so*, he thought. She had married a businessman. They had purchased their starter home and were saving to buy a larger one in the near future. They had both bought into the American Dream without realizing it. And although they were doing well by those standards, Diane sensed that Dick was struggling with some inner demons which made him restless and dissatisfied. He was thirty when he experienced *The Call*, and had years of education ahead of him before he could be ordained as an elder in the Methodist Church. Fortunately, the Methodist Church had a system to allow older candidates to enter the ministry and acquire their needed education. Dick obtained a License to Preach, and was assigned to a church in a small village near Jackson. This afforded them a place to live and provided a living wage to support the family while he completed his educational requirements.

After the pie and ice cream there was enough time for a family game and then a bedtime story with the girls. When they returned to the living room Dick told Diane he would have to go back later that night.

"When will that be?" Diane had learned that a minister's wife does not ask many questions. Confidentiality is vital to ministerial work. She would not inquire *what* or *whom*, but *when* was acceptable. This was one of only three nights when they could be together, to share the same bed, to share themselves. "When?" *was* a legitimate question.

"I have to be there at 11:00. It's something I need to check out." Dick realized as he said it that it sounded more than a little bit strange. His next words would sound even more odd: "I don't know for sure how long I'll be. Hopefully it will be no more than an hour."

"I'll be waiting up for you." Diane knew it would be foolish - even dangerous - for her to speculate. It could be that their children have to be put to bed and asleep before any counseling could be done. It could be that someone worked a late shift. Trust was called for, and trust would be given. "Try not to be too late. I'm a bit sleepy." She added this in a coquettish tone, hoping to encourage Dick to hasten whatever process he was engaged in.

Let's hope whatever it is that walks across that room doesn't wait long to do its thing. he muttered to himself as he drove back to Irene's. This has been a long day, and Dick wanted to get to bed . . . for a variety of reasons. He smiled in anticipation of some of those reasons. Dick arrived at the house, waited until Major roared, then opened the car door, walked quickly to the front door , and rang the bell. Irene looked through the small window, breathed a sigh of relief and let him in.

"Is Walter home yet?"

"No, this is his bowling night and he never gets home before midnight."

"With any luck, I should have heard the visitor and be gone by then, right?"

"That's what would usually happen."

Dick was feeling optimistic about this being a short visit, and being able to get home while Diane was still awake. She had been doing double duty as a mother and Head Start teacher/supervisor. It was good for her, though. Diane had been class valedictorian and a National Merit Scholar at the University of Michigan before he had talked her into leaving school to marry him. Dick realized she felt a bit cooped up and felt she was falling behind intellectually, as he went on for advanced degrees. The Head Start position gave her stimulus and extra money - both of which made her feel much better about herself. It did put an extra strain on her resources however. That, the kids, and the housework all served to take their toll.

Once at the house, Irene bid him a pleasant goodnight and retired to her bedroom. Dick settled himself in the sofa, turned off the lights. For a moment he reflected on what had become the Friday evening ritual with Cindy. *Normally she's a very confident, very competent, take charge type of person. Everyone needs a rock to lean on, I suppose*, he mused, recalling his own early struggles. *I suppose I am Cindy's for the moment. But she'll find stronger and better rocks along her path*. He thought this with a sense of confidence in her and a twinge of regret for himself. *It's kind of nice, though, being her hero for a while.* Then he switched his attention and began to mentally outline Sunday's sermon while he waited for whatever it was that might occur.

He had outlined his second point, complete with some illustrations he hoped would liven up the message, when he sensed a change in the room. *There really were sounds like the soft treading of footsteps moving across the carpet.*

Hold on there, Dick! he said to himself. *Don't let your imagination get the better of you.* He paused and listened more carefully. *Yes . . . . Yes! Those were footsteps!* Then he felt it: A Presence! It was palpable . . . like a cool, soft breeze lightly caressing his body. *Hold on, Richard, old man. There has to be some logical explanation for this.* Dick had always relied upon his keen intellect to break through barriers and solve the problems of life. As a kid he avoided classroom boredom by creating and solving problems of logic and math. He had always assumed he could earn straight A's if he was interested in such things. However, he had preferred being a Jack-of-all-trades: music, sports, and drama shared whatever might have been study time. Now, however, he was focused and – to his delight – learned that, indeed, he was quite capable of being an honor student. He was considered one of the top students, and many of his professors openly admired his analytical ability. He confidently told himself that this was just one more problem to solve. *Let's hold on, fella. Don't let your imagination run wild on you. Let's see. . . I hear a sound that is like footsteps. They're moving. Not stationary. The sounds moved from left to right.* He felt more in control now. His mind was taking charge. It was just a matter of time and he would find the answer. *What I felt was palpable. I felt it! Yes. I did. I felt it with my senses. My skin felt it! It wasn't some sixth sense. It was one of the good ol' five dependable ones. So it had to be something.* His mind was rushing now - racing toward the finish line. He was *confidant* of that.

Come on, guy. What are you missing? What could cause that in a hou-- Then it hit him. *The nights are cooler. The heat is on. When the furnace blower starts up the hot air moves through the ducts and causes them to expand. They crack as they expand. I've heard that many times before. The furnace is probably on the left of the basement and the heating ducts run to the right. That would make the sound move from left to right. Then the hot air pushes the lower lying cold air across the room toward the cold air return. That was the cool breeze I felt!* A little prompting and the imagination created a scenario of spooks circling the wagons - - - or whatever. Dick rose with a sense of victory. He had solved that one quickly enough. He did not know about the tipped over photographs and chairs, but he did know about the late night visitor. That was the ongoing problem, and his explanation should be enough to calm Irene's fears. She would laugh at herself when she learned what this disembodied spirit was. It should help her to keep her active imagination in check on those nights when Walter was out with the boys.

He closed the door quietly as he left, waited for Major's roar, then went to his car. It was still early. Diane would be awake.

CHAPTER 3

The next morning Dick went over to Irene's to explain in person what he had learned about the poltergeist. He smiled to himself as he drove, feeling a certain sense of smug satisfaction in having disposed of the poltergeist so quickly. If necessary, he was ready to demonstrate by turning the heat up and repeating the process in daylight.

Major didn't bark in daylight. He just snarled. That seemed good enough for Dick. This time he strode casually to the front door. This would probably be his last visit. *Let's let ol' Major know he doesn't strike fear into everyone's heart.* He smiled to himself as he realized the foolishness of the act. *Still, ego is ego, and we all do what we can to think well of ourselves.* He stepped on the porch rather jauntily and pressed the doorbell.

Walter answered, looking somewhat the worse for last night's wear. *Probably more beer than bowling,* Dick thought. Then he brightened. "Good morning, Walter. Is your charming wife around?" *Hold on, guy,"* he thought. *Don't get carried away. Remember you're the village pastor. Keep it humble and a bit more formal.* Walter grunted an affirmative and went inside, leaving Dick on the porch.

Irene quickly appeared. She seemed somewhat surprised to see Dick, but immediately made up for Walter's oversight by inviting him in. This time she went through the formality of offering a cup of tea or coffee.

"No thanks, Irene. I've just had breakfast." Dick wondered if this was a display for Walter's sake or if she actually was just a bit more relaxed. It didn't really matter, though. He assumed she had told Walter about the strange events she thought were occurring. She invited Dick into the living room, and Walter wandered off into the kitchen.

"Irene, I believe I've found your poltergeist." She raised her eyebrows in anticipation of the forthcoming explanation. *Keep it simple, but be specific and direct.* Dick thought, and he sat down on the sofa, in the exact place he had been the night before.

"When your furnace blower goes on, it pushes the hot air through the heating ducts, causing them expand with a light cracking sound. As the heat moves along, expanding the duct, the sound also moves, giving the impression of footsteps walking across the room. The cold air in the room rests near the floor and is pushed toward the return duct. When the cold air moves by you it can give a sense of a presence, particularly when you are alone in the quietness of evening. I felt it myself last night and at first thought it was a Presence. So don't be embarrassed." Dick paused to let this sink in. He felt, frankly, rather proud of himself that he solved it so quickly and had explained it so simply yet with enough specificity to satisfy any doubts.

Irene looked at him with what he took to be total disbelief: "Pastor Dick, this house sits on a slab of concrete. We don't have a basement. There are no heating ducts in the floor. There is no cold air return."

Walter returned from his sojourn in the kitchen, as if on cue, with a cup of coffee in his hand. He offered it to Dick, who took it absentmindedly as he sat, stunned. His thoughts sifted through last night's experience. He had *felt* something. He had *heard* something. There was no mistaking that. It had all seemed so simple - so logical. This had to make sense. *We don't live in a world where disembodied spirits stroll through private residences. That was some phenomenon out of the first century world. Certainly this kind of thing does not belong in the twentieth century.* He smiled weakly at Irene.

"Tell me more about this . . . experience."

She rested herself into the sofa. Walter wandered over and crowded in at the edge. The three of them sat for a moment, snuggled together in awkward silence. Then Irene spoke. As she did so, Dick felt himself sinking deeper and deeper into the rabbit hole.

Irene explained, "One night last week I was home alone and had this creepy feeling that I was *not* alone. I carefully checked every door to be certain they were locked. Walter has keys, so I did not worry about locking him out in case I was asleep when he returned." She paused and gave Walter what Dick sensed was a look of mild disapproval, which Walter did not seem to notice. "I am certain that I did not open any door. I just checked the locks." That seemed to Dick to be an odd distinction to make and he wondered where it was leading. He did not have to wonder long, however.

"Then I returned to the living room and began reading," Irene continued. After a few moments I was aware that Minnie was not with me. That was strange, I thought, because she always lays either right by my feet or on the sofa next to me." She paused to take a sip of her coffee, then picked up the narrative: "I called for her, but she did not respond. So I got up and began looking for her." Irene paused again, but this time not for coffee, but for effect. She pointed to the front door. "I heard scratching and whining at the door. I unlocked it - it *definitely* was locked - and there was Minnie! She almost fell in because she was up on her hind feet as though she were trying to push the door open." She paused again, reflecting upon the moment. "The poor thing was terrified. I held her on my lap and petted her and petted her. It took forever to calm her down. Pastor Dick, I have no idea how she could have gotten out of the house. The doors were locked. I never opened them. I was too nervous to have done that."

She paused now as though it was Dick's turn to say something. This was one of those rare moments when he could not find any words which seemed appropriate. Then he realized she wanted some assurance that he did not think she had somehow locked Minnie out without realizing it, and he finally broke the awkward silence by mumbling, "I believe you, Irene." Then he added, trying to be truthful, "I have no idea what happened, but I believe you that it happened as you said."

Walter just sat, looking blank   Dick wondered whether he had heard the story too many times, or if he dismissed it as imagination . . . or if he was thinking about the high game he bowled last night.

CHAPTER 4

Monday morning arrived all too early. The entire family had stayed up quite late on Sunday in an attempt to make up for some of their lost time together. This week Leonard would leave his pickup truck with Diane as it was Dick's turn to drive the carpool. They were still finishing breakfast as Leonard pulled up in front of the parsonage, jumped out, and strode quickly to the door. Dick was fond of Leonard. Whenever he thought of Peter the fisherman, who followed Jesus, he pictured Leonard: six foot tall, raw boned, almost black hair, with rough-hewn good looks. Leonard had studied to be a state police officer, but had become a farmer until he, also, had felt an irresistible call to preach. He was ten years Dick's senior. Even though he was not a scholar he possessed a good quality mind and a steadiness born of experience which Dick appreciated. They made an interesting pair: bright scholar and wise farmer. Their time together was always a precious time for both of them.

"Leonard, what do you know about disembodied spirits?" Dick asked as he put his car in gear and they turned into the highway.

"Never met one. I know something about the Holy Spirit, about distilled spirits, and school spirit," he laughed. "Did you find one lying around the parsonage?" he chuckled.

Dick decided that this was not going to lead anywhere, so he quickly changed the subject. "Nah, I was just curious." Let's stay with the Holy Spirit. Do you believe it is somehow bestowed upon you, or does it rise within you when awakened?"

Leonard licked his chops with this. He enjoyed this theological banter. Dick always raised questions that the professors overlooked. After a weekend of ministering to a congregation of very nice - but essentially poorly educated people, it was good to get his thinking cap on before they arrived at seminary.

"Scripture says the Spirit comes upon you, Dick. It's something that Jesus promised and God gives." He waited, knowing that Dick was going to pursue a thought that was new and would somehow make sense.

"I know that most people experience it as coming upon them Leonard, but they describe it as 'filling them.' Perhaps what they experience is actually a bursting forth from within. Scripture also says - way back in Genesis - that God breathed into Adam - which meant humanity, right?" He did not wait for a response. "We both know that the Hebrew and the Greek word for breath and spirit are the same, right? God only did that to Adam. All the other creatures he merely created - but did not breathe his breath - or spirit - into them. That means that humanity is inspirited. What if the spirit was blown into us and merely waits to be awakened in its entirety?" Dick paused to let this sink in.

Leonard grinned. This would be fun. He decided to take the traditional path, to challenge Dick. "What difference would it make? Why argue with Scripture?"

"For one thing it means that the Spirit of God is available to everyone. It blows away the old Calvinistic theory of predestination. You don't have to wait passively, hoping you will be chosen to receive it. It's there somewhere inside you, just waiting to burst forth, to revitalize you and recreate your whole understanding of what life is about." Dick was on a roll. Leonard knew he needed no prodding, so he just nodded.

"Jesus' call was to repent, believe the good news and enter the Kingdom. We know that the meaning of repent has been distorted over the years. It originally meant to transform your mind - or understanding - usually after reflection. When someone actually begins to understand the message of Jesus this tears down all the little defenses - clears away all the distortions created by society - and allows the Spirit to burst forth into a new freedom - a new life. Thus the saying, 'born again' which really better translates as 'born from above.'" Dick leaned back. It was now Leonard's turn.

Leonard was willing to give Dick his point, but had to inquire, "Okay, it's a workable theory, Dick, but why bother? You're not going to change people's way of thinking."

"I know that, Leonard. There's no need to change anyone's mind if what they believe works for them. I'm after the skeptic - the bright unbeliever who can't accept the idea of some God-out-there capriciously bestowing his spirit - and thus his favor upon only a portion of humanity. I want to reach those thoughtful persons who either were never trained to think in the traditional manner, or who rejected it somewhere along the way. What's wrong with that?"

Leonard only chuckled. "Nothing, Dick. Nothing at all. Good luck."

They both lapsed into silence, reflecting upon the conversation in their separate ways. Leonard appreciated Dick's mind and his zeal. For himself, Leonard just wanted to complete his seminary work, take a small church somewhere, and preach to ordinary people about life's ordinary problems, assuring them of God's love. He loved people and had the knack for making them trust him. His training to be a state trooper had just been a diversion to his real calling. He knew that. *The past is only prelude*, he thought, recalling something he had heard or read long ago.

For his part, Dick had slipped back into the events at Irene's. *How could the dog have gotten out of the house? Was a window left open? Danny had been in bed. Irene was cautious. She certainly would have found an open window. She would be thorough in her quest for safety. And those pictures and chairs? Danny wouldn't have thought to do that. Besides he was too short to have reached the top shelf - even if he used a chair as a ladder.*

Dick fretted. There always was a logical answer to every event. Yet somehow he felt he might be experiencing something that did not fit into his understanding of how life worked.

He would soon find out how right this hunch was.

CHAPTER 5

The seminary sat on the edge of the Northwestern University campus in Evanston. The architecture was what might be called "more or less Gothic." The central building was an imposing gray stone structure, as were two of the older dorms. The newest building, however, reflected the architecture of the times: red brick with low, sweeping lines - constructed more for utility than appearance. Dick had lived there his first year, but moved to the third floor of one of the older dorms in order to have some quiet and privacy. Although he was gregarious by nature, there were just too many drop-ins and requests for help with homework to allow him the focus he felt he needed. *I've got only four years to pick up all the tools I'm going to need for a lifetime of ministry*, he told himself. *Best I forget about the social stuff for a while.*

Seminary was an amazing arcade of learning for Dick. *Everything you wanted to know about God,* he thought. He relished the classes with "the true thinkers" on the faculty staff. Most professors had good minds. Some were about average. Then there were those select few whose intellects shone like spotlights beaming across blackened skies, lighting up the darkness with flashes of insight and understanding. "Thou shall worship the Lord your God with all your heart, mind, soul and strength." That's what the Carpenter of Nazareth had said. Dick had some understanding of heart and strength. He knew that. Not so much of soul. He admitted that, as well.

Mind, however, was his domain. *Do what you're good at*. he had told himself, so for those precious hours in the classroom of "the true thinkers," he bathed in their brilliance and sponged up every drop of knowledge they let fall from their lips. It did not really matter what the subject of the course was. The true thinkers taught one to think, to delve beneath the surfaces and understand - really understand - what gave rise to the words, the creeds, the decisions and actions which shaped the Church. Ordinary minds merely taught the facts as they were presented and required regurgitation of those facts for their exams ("Academic Vomit," is what he called it). The below average thinkers taught "Test Passing 101." They knew what was required from their field of study in order to pass the Comprehensive Exams. This is what they taught. Good soldiers, doing their part to see that there would be a steady flow of qualified pastors to serve the church. The trouble lay in that their students may emerge as qualified by Church standards, but that did not mean they were in any way equipped to handle the difficult questions which invariably rose in people's minds in times of disaster or crisis. He had already encountered them. Pre-packaged responses do not begin to satisfy the hearts or souls – much less the minds of those caught in crisis and tragedy.

"It was God's Will." makes me sick every time I hear some damn fool utter it. Thought Dick. *It's always said with a pious expression, as though that should be accepted. What it does is preclude any further discussion, if the listener has any sense. Later, that same fool who gave the answer will call upon the people to love and trust this deity who destroyed their lives.* He looked over to Leonard, wondering if

he should bring that idea up for discussion. Then he dismissed the idea as quickly as he thought it. Leonard felt the same way but he would defend them as having loving hearts and good intentions.

Dick's spare time was spent in study. One hour for volley ball in the evening. No time for idle chit chat. One shot at gathering in all the knowledge needed for a lifetime. Fill the mind. Expand the mind. Hone the mind like a sword.

Theological conversation was allowed - even sought out. God is infinite. Mind is finite. Dick welcomed "the true students" into his world. They helped with the filling, the expansion, the honing. Truth could set one free. Knowledge was truth. "Love the Lord your God with . . . all your *mind*." Yes. That's what the Rabbi from Galilee said. Rabbi - teacher. If there was more, he could deal with that after seminary. Seminary was for the mind. Dick might speculate about spirit - holy or otherwise. But for him religion was an academic issue - a matter of *understanding*.

The school held chapel four days out of the five. Wednesday, for some reason was left vacant. With so many worship choices, the students tended to read the "menu" to see who the special of the day might be. Some professors filled the room to overflowing. Some only managed to garner those who were in their classes that term and were afraid not to be seen. Dick's criterion was clear: "The true thinkers." Worthy sermons stimulated the mind. When the others spoke, Dick could be found in the library.

Once, when prowling through ancient writings he encountered a statement made by Thomas Aquinas, the brilliant medieval theologian: "The Holy Spirit remains a holy mystery." Aquinas had arrived at this conclusion after years of thoughtful research on that subject - and only that subject. Increasingly, Dick became convinced that the term "spirit" was, at best, a confused term, alternately denoting emotion and some vague attempt to experience divinity. It was one of those terms preachers employed to leap over difficult issues. Poorly defined. Pious in pronouncement. A perfect weasel word.

That's why Irene's poltergeist was beginning to bother him - haunt him, really. If what was happening in the house was some kind of spirit - if it was Irene's dead mother - then what does that say about this word *spirit* and the *realm of the spirit*? Some part of him wanted to dwell on that and explore it. Some other portion resisted, like some of his parishioners who put off seeing their doctors about some nagging symptom . . . for fear of learning what they really do not want to know.

CHAPTER 6

The members of the carpool were feeling particularly jubilant as they loaded themselves into the cramped sedan to begin the long trek home.

"Homeward bound!" shouted Ken, as he slammed the door shut.

"Yes, sir!" Dick responded, as he edged the car from its tight parking spot and onto Sheridan Road. Dick liked Ken. He was the youngest of the group, a former salesman who had felt the calling into the ministry. Now, with two young children he was serving a small, village congregation, living in a somewhat run down house and having the time of his life. Ken was bright and energetic: Always upbeat and positive. People were drawn to him. He was sure to do well in his new profession.

"Goodbye, ol' pregnant pig," Bob muttered as they drove past the Northwestern library. "Pregnant Pig" was the term their professor of preaching, Dr. George Buttrick, employed to describe this architectural absurdity. Actually, if one employed just a smidgeon of imagination it really did resemble an enormous pregnant pig lying on its back - belly up. It was a bit of the light-hearted humor the seminary students employed to jostle the Northwestern students. In the same vein, Northwestern students referred to the seminary as East Jesus Tech.

"Head for Burger King," ordered Bob. There were a couple of different routes which could be taken through Chicago at that time of day. The choice was usually made to accommodate someone's appetite for the fast food outlets on the way.

"Home of the Whopper!" Leonard grinned. "I'd love that sign for my front yard." Everyone chuckled at Leonard's earthy humor.

"If the congregation could hear our conversations, they'd take us off those pedestals wouldn't they?" Ken offered.

"We'd all be more comfortable if they did. Right?" Dick responded over his shoulder, as he kept his eyes on the increasing traffic. "This aura of piety so many want to bestow on us is just so much skubalon!" Dick enjoyed using New Testament Greek which had broadened his understanding of Scripture in many ways. The Greek was koine - common - nothing like the eloquent flowing English of the King James, still treasured and adored by so many of his congregation. Some writers, such as Luke and whoever wrote Hebrews, were rather eloquent. Mostly, however, the writers possessed the earthy vocabulary and syntax of the average Joe of their time. *Skubalon* was a term used by good old St. Paul. The lexicon politely termed it *dung*. Dick, enjoyed explaining it as "Today's Latinized term would be *crap*." The Greek gave him a new feel for Scripture.

This briefly opened the door for a discussion of the varying views people have about clergy.

"Most of the guys treat me like a regular Joe, but most of the ladies especially the older ones - act as though I'm something special." Bob said with a shrug. He'd traveled the world as an astronomer prior to entering the ministry. Bob had seen and tasted a great variety of people and attitudes. He had come to accept the diversity.

"I wish they'd put me on a pedestal." Ron said with a soft chuckle. Normally Ron didn't enter into the rough and tumble discussions that anything ecclesiastical or theological was certain to become. He usually was content either to listen quietly or to entertain himself with his own daydreams. Ron was one of those lost persons still searching for enough pieces of himself to figure out who he was and become that person with confidence. A nice enough guy, but easily lost in a crowd of three. Some of the group harbored the belief that Ron had drifted in the ministry because it offered a guaranteed employment and a decent minimum salary. Too many polite, passive young men had found their way into this ecclesiastical refuge of late. It was no wonder that the Methodist church was sagging in membership. No one in the group talked about Ron in this regard, however. There was some tacit understanding that they kept any negative opinions about one another to themselves. If they were to manage carpooling for three or four years together it was essential that there be no cliques, exclusions or scapegoats.

"Yeah, you and Rodney Dangerfield," Ken said with a laugh. "No respect!" "Wasn't it Jesus who said a prophet is not without honor, except in his own town and with his own people?"

"Don't sweat it, Ron. You're in good company." Bob closed that diversion, and refocused the discussion. "We've all had those awkward moments when we are introduced to somebody's friend, and they say, 'Watch your language. He's a minister' or 'man of God' - or - some term to say, 'This guy's different. He's not quite like us.'" Everyone nodded in silent agreement. Then Leonard broke the silence with a question: "Why do you think that is? I mean, everyone who knows me knows I farmed - and still farm a bit." He paused - - "My asparagus crop, you know. It pays for this seminary thing."

"People need us to be different. That's why" Dick let this sink in, then continued. "We are the God Makers."

"The what?" It sounded like a chorus. Everyone - even Ron - had chimed in as though on cue. Dick smiled to himself. He enjoyed the shock and teach approach. First get their attention. Then become reasonable. Often the best approach is to ask the correct questions. The listener then either will find the answer for himself, or at least be open to the answer offered.

"Okay, think about this - and anyone - anyone at all - give an answer. There are no wrong ones. No pass/fail. Ready? Without waiting for a response, he jumped in:

"What do you know - or think you know about God? You don't have to answer right now. If this idea is going to have any chance to penetrate into your present theological systems, it must have time. Like Jesus' idea of the seed growing silently, let the idea lay around in your mind for awhile. Ask yourselves honestly how you came to believe what you believe about God, Jesus, Sin, Salvation - all those doctrinal issues we're being taught to pass along. Then also ask yourselves what you really know and believe - deep down where it counts. We'll pick this up next Monday, okay?"

The others seemed to accept this. At least it would be a break in the normal drive routine. Maybe, what Dick was proposing had some parts that could open up some new understanding. At any rate, the idea of a good rough and tumble debate whetted their appetites. Leonard, Bob and Ken began making lists of what they knew - or thought they knew. Ron closed his eyes and began his customary nap home.

After Ron and Ken had been dropped off at their homes, the car continued along the back roads until they reached the corner where Carol was waiting to pick up Bob. Bob hopped out, opened the trunk, grabbed his bag, waved and gave the obligatory, "Give them *The Word* - See you Monday." Dick slipped the car in gear and drove over to Highway 12. The term highway was a misnomer by the day's standards. Michigan Avenue described it more accurately. It once served as the state highway, wending its way through every town between Detroit in the eastern corner to Three Rivers at the western border. I-94 had long-ago replaced it. Its traffic moved along the divided one-way roads at seventy plus mph on smooth two and three lanes of limited access, smooth pavement. Old 12 was what the carpool had to travel for most of Michigan. That was the route which held the small towns with their small, student-supply-pastor churches.

This was the long stretch of the trek which Leonard and Dick enjoyed most. They were fond of one another but rarely saw each other while at the seminary. Different classes and different dormitories created distances which they both tacitly realized was good for their relationship. Dick was the scholar; Leonard was the more-average student. Academics were not their proper meeting ground. Their souls merged at different areas. Both had been in the military. Both had been reasonably successful in their other lives. They understood the struggles of making payrolls and taking care of business while trying to maintain families and friendships. More than that, however - they had *clicked!* It happens now and then. The moment they met, they intuitively liked and trusted one another. This is the bond which raises friendships to the level of intimates: This ability to share openly their thoughts, their failures and their secret aspirations, knowing they would be understood and never disclosed.

"Len, my friend, I am struggling with this whole issue of spirituality." Dick offered, pausing to decide whether to wait for a response or proceed. The silence told him Leonard was waiting for more input before wanting to answer, so he continued: The way the profs talk about *spiritual* is like a synonym for *emotional.* The group that meets for what they call spiritual development are nerds - semi-outcasts who don't seem to fit in well. That doesn't serve to recommend trying to get whatever it is they think they're after." He let this sit. It was time now for Leonard to answer. They drove on along the twisting and narrow highway for a few more miles. Then Leonard spoke: "Dick, could it be that you're living too much out of your head, and not enough out of your heart and soul?" He paused, then added, "Remember, we were told to love the Lord our God with all our heart, mind, soul *and* strength. It wasn't either/or."

Dick nodded his agreement, but was not about to give up his point. "You may recall that Plato proposed that the mind leads the soul. You can't give yourself over to something your mind cannot accept. We've both seen that too many times with people caught up with some overly-zealous religious group. They say the words, but they neither understand them nor believe them - - deep down where it matters. And when something bad happens to them they fall apart. Oh, they may fake it for a while, smiling and saying 'It was God's will,' but inside, they are disintegrating."

I know all that, Dick. But I'm talking about you going off on a head trip. It wasn't your understanding that caused you to sell your home and enter the ministry. You experienced something that you believed was real. Right?"

"You're right, Len, but now and then I wonder if it was some sort of divine encounter, or just some sort of mid-life crisis. It doesn't make sense that I actually heard the voice of God. It sort of makes me feel like a Moses wannabe - just minus the bush."

Leonard grinned at that. Well, Dick, like Moses, you're going to lead a lot of people - either into a wilderness - or the Promised Land. You better figure out which way you're going . . . before you go much further."

That seemed to end that conversation, and they both sank into silence until the car arrived at the parsonage. Len took his luggage, waved goodbye and drove off to begin a new weekend of work.

The home-coming ritual was lovingly repeated: Deb first, then Diane, then into the next room to draw Cindy back into the family circle. Saturday would be soon enough to visit Irene.

After dinner, they gathered around the cleared table to play a board game and enjoy a quiet family evening. While Deb set up the board, Dick wondered how Irene's poltergeist was doing.

He was soon to learn it was doing quite well, thank you.

Chapter 7

This time, Irene was with two neighbors. Dick could see the eagerness on their faces. The niceties of coffee and/or cookies were by-passed. Obviously it has been a more-than- interesting week, and Dick was about to learn just how unusual it had been for each of the ladies.

Rita lived across the street. She was a rather attractive brunette in her late twenties. Her husband was an engineer and she was a stay-at-home mom with two children: one still in the crib. Linda lived next door. She was about thirty, average height, average weight, average looks: The kind who would be difficult to describe. Obviously they had agreed upon the sequence. Irene spoke first:

"When I realized this *thing* might be my mother, I called my grandmother and told her what was happening. She then told me that my mother had called for me one evening while I was still in nurse's training. Even though mother was very ill, grandmother decided that I needed my rest and she would wait until morning to call me. However, mother slipped into coma and died before morning. 'Perhaps she is trying to tell you something,' grandmother said. 'Get an ouija board,' so I did. As you probably know, it requires two people to use one, so I asked Rita to be my partner for this."

At this, Rita jumped in and began her tale:

"I left my son, Johnny, and Irene's Danny to play in the living room. You can watch the house from this room, so I figured it would be okay to leave them playing. The baby was safely tucked away in her crib in my bedroom, so I did not worry." She paused and shook her head as if giving some signal to herself, then she continued: "Nothing happened for a long time. I sat there feeling totally ridiculous, even wondering if I should start nudging the marker to make Irene feel better. Then suddenly I felt it moving and it was all I could do just to keep my hands on it." She paused again, shaking her head, and this time Dick understood it to be a gesture of disbelief. "It spelled b–a–b–y. then it paused and continued d–a–n–g–e–r. Baby danger. 'What do you mean?' I asked – beginning to feel a sense of panic rise up in me. Then it repeated itself: b–a–b–y - - - d–a–n–g–e–r. That did it for me. I jumped up and rushed home. Everything looked fine. Johnny and Danny were playing in the living room as though nothing was wrong. They even looked startled to see me rush by. I opened the bedroom door and looked in the crib." Here she paused. "You know those large center boards we put in the dining room tables to make more room for guests?" Dick nodded, but that was unnecessary. Rita's question was purely rhetorical. With a look of total disbelief she continued: "It should have been behind the dresser, leaning against the wall" (another pause) "IT WAS LYING IN THE CRIB – RIGHT NEXT TO THE BABY! Some one – or some thing – had taken that heavy table board from behind the dresser and had placed it in my daughter's crib!" She paused again to let this sink in. Dick mentally reeled back at this news. It made no sense to him at all, but obviously this is what happened. Rita had no reason to lie about such a thing. He sat stunned, waiting for Rita to continue. "That did it for me. I told Irene, 'You keep the ouija board if you want, but I'm not going near it again.'" With this, she slumped back in her chair, as if she had just completed a ten kilometer race.

Now it was Linda's turn: "So of course, Irene came on over next door to good old Linda's. She didn't tell me about Rita's experience." She looked at Irene to give assurance. "That's okay. I would have helped out anyway. That's what friends and neighbors do." With this, she exchanged smiles with Irene, then continued with her tale. "Like with Rita, we sat holding the marker with nothing happening and me feeling like an idiot, but willing to stay with it because of Irene's concern. Suddenly it started moving on us. At first I thought it was Irene. I mean the strength of the movement was too great not to have been caused by someone. It wasn't one of those little, 'Oh, gee, I think it might be moving things.' Someone – or some *thing* was making that little sucker move!" She looked straight at Dick to emphasize her point. "I mean something other than me or Irene was pushing that marker around the board!"

Dick got caught up in the tension and jumped in: "What was it saying?" He had passed the point of disbelief – though he was in no way going to admit the presence of a spirit. He knew that these ladies were telling the truth about what they believed happened. Their earnestness was obvious. Dick just had to dig beneath their remembrances to figure out what in the name of -well – anything sacred would do - was actually happening in that house.

"It spelled out disconnected words: Chicago – baby – nurse – Rose – thunderbird – motel – Denver. This made absolutely no sense to us, but we wrote them down, then sat and waited for the marker to move again. Nothing happened, and eventually we relaxed our hold on the marker and just chit chatted." She paused as though this was the end of the story. Then she began again: "The radio had been playing music in the background and we really hadn't noticed it, but suddenly a voice broke in announcing that some baby that had been kidnapped from a hospital in Chicago had been found in the Thunderbird Motel in Denver, Colorado. The kidnapper was a nurse named Rose."

Dick recalled the incident. The Chicago papers and radios had been filled with the story of this baby being kidnapped – even before it had been foot printed. It had not mentioned the missing nurse, even though the police must have been aware of that. Then months later just last week, in fact, the baby had been found in some motel in Denver and the kidnapper had been a nurse from that hospital. The name "Rose" sounded about right. *What in the name of - anything – was going on here?* Dick questioned silently. Outwardly he merely nodded calmly and allowed Linda to continue her tale.

"Well, Irene and I just sat there staring at each other. Irene said something about her mother always having a great interest in needy children, but that made no sense to me at the time. I just figured that whatever we were supposed to have accomplished with that darned ouija board had been accomplished, and I headed back home." She paused again; looked directly at Dick in a way one looks when telling a mystery story; then continued: "Here is where it really got interesting. When I got back home my front screen door was locked. I checked the back door and it was locked, too." She looked at Dick again with that sense of mystery. "I was locked out of my house! I had no key. There was no way that screen door could have accidentally locked itself. Come. Let me show you."

She arose and Dick followed to the house next door. "See!" Linda announced triumphantly. "Check for yourself. That door simply could not have locked itself." Dick looked at the lock. It was one of those simple hook locks that you have to push into the eye screw to fasten it. Dick checked it twice. It required some direct pressure to make it secure. It absolutely could not have fallen into place.

"That did it for me!" Linda said. I told Irene that I didn't know what was going on in her house and what that board was about, but I was through with it."

Dick returned to Irene's house in a daze. He simply asked her, "Was that it? Anything else happen?"

"No," Irene replied. That was it for last week."

"Let me think about this," Dick responded. Then turned and headed back to his car. Nothing was making sense, here. Nothing at all. *Why would whoever was making that board move want to scare off Linda's neighbors so she can't use the board?* As he drove back home, Dick mused that he wished he had never become involved in this. Yet there had been no way to avoid it. Irene was one of his parishioners; she had been troubled and it was his duty to try to help. He just did not have any idea now what kind of help he might be able to give.

He continued to search his mind for some logical explanation for all that was happening.

ESP might have been involved in what the ouija board was doing. But how could that table board move – and the screen door lock - - - ?

When he walked through the parsonage door he felt relieved to return to the other side of that looking glass and spend some time with Diane and the girls.

CHAPTER 8

"You're quiet today, Dick. Was it a tough weekend?" Leonard finally broke the silence after they had been driving for half an hour.

Dick smiled, "You wouldn't believe it if I told you."

That was enough for Leonard. He respected other people's privacy, and it was obvious to him that Dick did not wish to talk about whatever it was that was troubling him. This was one of the qualities Dick respected in him. It is what made him a valued friend and a good pastor. Knowing when to intervene and when to stay out of it was a rare quality.

"Are we going to have that "God Makers" free-for-all when the other get aboard?" Leonard changed the subject – not just to change it but to redirect Dick's thinking away from whatever was troubling him.

"Good heavens, Len, I forgot about it. Give me a few more minutes to get some thoughts together and we'll start up after we get Bob and Ken."

Dick thought: *God Makers! God Makers! We are the God Makers! What was I trying to say? Oh yes: Why do people treat us clergy as something different – something special? We know – or at least I hope we know – that we are no different – no better – than anybody else. We just happen to have had this calling to try to tell people about God and his plan or hope – or love - for us. What I wrestle with is how we think we know any more about that than anyone else? Sure, we have special classes and some great teachers, but where does their understanding come from? I guess that's the place to start this theological brawl.* That settled, Dick relaxed and asked Leonard, "Anything good happen to you over the weekend?"

The light-hearted banter continued until Bob and Ken were tucked in the back seat, then Ken spoke: "All right, great guru. Why are we the God Makers?"

"I guess I could ask you that same question: What makes us the God Makers? What gives us the right to stand in the pulpits and say, 'Thus says the Lord'? That's what we do every time we preach a sermon. In one way or another we are saying, 'This is what God requires of you' – or 'This is what God is like' – or 'this is how God will help you – or act for you – or judge you.'" Dick stopped to let this idea soak in. "Among all the professions in the world we are the ones most likely to break the fourth commandment." This caused the others to silently begin counting the commandments, but before they could arrive at the fourth, Dick continued: "'You shall not take the name of the Lord in vain.' Fellas, that has nothing to do with what someone says when his golf drive makes a duck hook into a pond – or hits the thumb instead of the nail with his hammer.. That stuff is just bad manners. Taking the Lord's name in vain means using God's name for one's own vain purpose."

Bob decided to play devil's advocate and jumped in: "Wait a minute, Dick, every sermon is based on Scripture. A sermon just interprets that Scripture to give it meaning in life situations."

"Yeah, I know what they say they teach us to do, Bob. Exegetical analysis of Scripture – We read meaning *out* of Scripture. Sounds good – sure – but we all know we are just as likely to be eisegetical – to read the meaning we want to find *into* Scripture. Can any of us here honestly say that we have not done that at one time or another – to make a political point – or justify some preconceived notion?"

Leonard chuckled at this: "It's that old story about the Bible-quoting mechanic who cheated this guy passing through town, and when asked how he could justify having done so, said, "Well – 'He was a stranger, so I took him in.'"

"It makes a good joke, but we've all done it – in one way or another. We grab a passage out of context and make it mean what we want it to mean. Right?"

There was a general nodding of heads and affirmative murmers.

Ken broke the silence: "What's that got to do with our being God Makers, though? All-in-all, we try to be true to Scripture. We proclaim the God revealed by Jesus Christ. We don't make God up."

"Maybe not."   Dick paused for effect . . . "But someone did, and we add our touch."

Dick couldn't have created a stronger reaction if he had put a broom handle in a hornet's nest. Everyone jumped at once, but Dick settled on Leonard's words, "Just how do you figure that?"

"Okay, just for openers, I'll start with the obvious: Jesus tells of the Great Judgment where the unrighteous are sent to hell or cast into the darkness in Matthew 25, right?"   There was general agreement shown by nods and grunts.   "He also tells of the Prodigal's father who unconditionally welcomed his son. Right?" Again there was agreement. "That kid wasn't sorry. He didn't come home because he missed or loved his Father. He just had no other place to go. Yet his father didn't make him grovel or promise to repay or put any restriction on him at all. He just rejoiced." Dick paused to let the contrast begin to sink in. "We all know the story wasn't about the son. Jesus was telling us about God, the Waiting Father. So which is it: punishment or forgiveness? Hell for screwing up, or unconditional acceptance of who we are? . . . or do we alternate the two to fit our purpose?"

This was met by silence. Each one sat quietly reflecting on the truth of Dick's words – feeling somewhat condemned. Each knew that he had alternated between speaking of God's unconditional loving forgiveness and placing all sorts of conditions on that love.

"Come on, guys . . . we all know the hell-fire and damnation preachers who literally try to scare the hell out of their parishioners. We also know the universalists who proclaim that God will redeem everyone. They both can't be right. But the people who attend their churches accept those images of God. Those preachers shape the God worshiped in their churches."

About this time, they were arriving at the corner where Ron would be waiting. Dick decided that he did not want to take the time to bring him up to speed on their discussion. "Let's just let it sit there until Friday, shall we? But do give it some thought. What image of God do we paint with our sermons? Is it clear or blurred? Is it loving or judgmental? Is it something we have been taught or something we have tested and believe?"

Ron was waiting at the corner. He threw his bag into the trunk, and opened the back door. "Hi, guys! What's happening?"

"Nothing much," Bob answered. We were just discussing some of the things they've been trying to teach us at Mother Garrett."

Each settled back into his own thoughts. Ron curled up in his corner to take one last nap. He explained hastily that he had been up late, making a hospital call, sitting and praying with young parents while their little girl was undergoing an emergency appendectomy. Dick watched him in his rear view mirror. *Ron certainly was not a scholar, and he probably was not much of a preacher,* he thought to himself. *He has a pastor's heart though. His people might not get a clear image of God from his preaching and teaching. They would, however, experience a deep, caring love from this timid, quiet man. He would love them and they would love him, and maybe – just maybe – that's what this ministering thing really is about.*

Leonard started singing with his wonderfully deep baritone-bass voice: "When you're a long, long way from home . . . .." Ken added his clear tenor tones. Bob quietly began working on his Sunday's sermon. Dick observed the town limit sign and unconsciously thought, Two hours and twenty three minutes to go. Then he, too, started to mull over his next Sunday's sermon. Driving was a good time for that. *How in blazes did that table board get into that crib? Those little kids couldn't have done that. And how did that screen door lock itself from the inside – and why?* He kept being dragged back through that looking glass . . . and it was uncomfortable not having any of the answers.

CHAPTER 9

It had been a busy week at seminary: Mid terms and major papers had been due. There had been no time to prepare the mandatory Sunday sermon or whatever weekend classes were to be taught. Consequently, the ride back was crowded with silence as each rider mentally wrote and rewrote his sermon. Dick's thoughts were only interrupted by an occasional familiar sign which automatically proclaimed itself as *an hour and a half from home and Diane and the girls.* Irene and her ghostly visitor never crept into his consciousness.

Dick pulled up to the parsonage. He and Leonard got out – Dick heading for the door and Leonard heading for his truck. Diane had left the keys in the ignition, ready for him to depart immediately. He had another half hour to go and it was already quite dark – and well past supper time.

The Friday evening ritual was repeated: First Debbie, next Diane, then – finally - Cindy was lovingly coaxed back from within her fears into the life of the now-resumed family.

Dick had learned that whatever was happening with Irene and her unwanted guest could wait until Saturday morning. This allowed the much-anticipated, much needed family evening . . . and also avoided meeting Major in the dark.

After breakfast, Dick called Irene to see whether there was any reason to drop by the house. As suspected, there was. "You need to come here to see this," was her response to his query. He debated for a moment whether he should shave. There were no weddings or funerals scheduled. There were no hospital calls or meetings that night. Dick really liked to give his face a rest and let his face go scrubby when he had the chance. He peered in the mirror, trying to figure out if it would pass. Then he thought about Walter: *That guy looks like he was born with five o'clock shadow. If Irene can take that every day, she certainly can stand this stubble for a few minutes.* Having thus convinced and justified himself, he slipped on a respectable shirt and headed over to see the latest chapter in this real live soap opera.

Major was nowhere to be seen, and Dick had stopped worrying about him in the daylight. He walked quickly to the door, rang the bell and waited for a brief moment before Irene opened the door and invited him in. "Come into the bedroom. I need to show you something." Given different circumstances, Dick would have declined, but it never crossed his mind that Irene had any concern other than her unwanted house guest. "This morning Danny came into the bedroom, still half asleep. It was about seven o'clock and Walter and I were just beginning to wake up. Danny likes to come in and cuddle on Saturdays, when we have time for that. But before he could climb under the covers, he turned – like someone had called him. He sort of staggered over to the wall, here." At this, Irene strode over to a portion of the wall at the foot of their double bed, and she pointed at a spot of the wall. "Right here, there was a small, very bright light shining. Danny stood in front of it as though it was speaking to him. Then suddenly the light jumped over to this spot." At this, Irene walked over to a place at the side of the bed. "Danny just looked at it, and nodded . . . as if to say, 'Goodbye.'" Walter had walked into the bedroom as Irene was telling his story. He said nothing. He just nodded, as though to affirm that this is what he saw, as well.

Dick reflected on this – then got sidetracked. *Walter just nods.* He thought. *He never speaks. He just nods – and walks around. Irene isn't losing a thing with him being gone so much.* Then he quickly got his mind back on the subject. There was a window just next to the headboard of the bed. An outside light could have shone on the wall where Danny first saw the light. *Could some neighbor be playing tricks on them?* Dick asked himself. Then he walked over to the window and looked at the place at the side of the bed where the light had jumped. There was no way that same light could have shone there. Dick should have been getting accustomed to this, but the thought caused his skin to crawl again. *There has to be some logical explanation to all this, but darned if I can find it!* He had that same feeling of frustration as when some complicated puzzle finally wears him down and he's forced to look up the answer to see if there really is one.

He rubbed his head as though trying to clear his brain, and he realized his shoulders were drooping. *Boy, am I ever giving this family a feeling of confidence,* he thought ironically. For some reason Irene had assumed that this "man of God" would be able to cast out whatever spirit had invaded her home. For a moment his mind ran back to the carpool conversations about God makers. While still trying to get hold of this problem, Irene presented another:

"Pastor Dick, I don't think I told you that I am pregnant again. Well yesterday I had a doctor's appointment and was supposed to take along a urine sample. I had made one, but had not put the cap on it (mainly because I had forgotten where I had put it). I supposed I had left it in the bathroom, so I just placed the bottle on the dresser and planned to get the top after I had finished dressing." She paused and gave another one of those you-won't-believe-this looks. Dick braced himself to try to appear calm and casual about what she was going to say. *If I can't solve this, at least I can try to be a calming presence*, he thought as she continued.

"The bottle lifted up – all by itself. Then it slowly spun itself in a circle," with this she made a large circle, moving upward and to her right, then downward and to her left, until the imaginary circle was complete. "Not a drop fell out," she said in disbelief. Dick automatically looked toward Walter, who just nodded agreement. "Walter tried to explain that the liquid was held in by centrifugal force. I told him that was not possible, but you know Walter -" Dick nodded tacit agreement although he realized he actually did not know Walter at all. "He had to demonstrate that he was right, so he picked it up and started to show me how that could happen." At this she glared quickly at Walter. Dick felt a twinge of pleasure that Irene stood up to this red-necked chauvinist at least on occasion. "Well, of course he spilled it all over the carpet." Dick hastily glanced over to the dresser and noticed the deep-piled rug. "He cleaned it up while I went back to the bathroom and fortunately was able to make another sample." She glared at Walter again, and

Walter lowered his eyes and nodded to acknowledge that this was indeed what had happened.

"Let me think about this, Irene. I am going to have to do some research." With this, Dick turned and beat a retreat to the door. He had absolutely no idea of what kind of research he could do, or where he could turn for any help. If he told his professors, he knew some of them at least would think him a gullible fool. "Guess what our Wells Scholar does with his weekends – He's a ghost buster!"

Just the week before, the local paper had printed a major story about a family in Jackson that claimed to be haunted by a ghost. It had created such a furor that they had to get a court order to keep the curious and the wanna-be-exorcists away. People had broken down their fence, trampled their shrubs, and generally made themselves obnoxious pests. When he had read of their problems he promised Irene he would never divulge her name or her story to anyone. *So what do I do now?* he asked himself. He was so wrapped up in this combination of confusion, frustration and helplessness that if Major had been sitting on his car hood he would not have noticed.

He drove directly home, but try as he might, this time he could not get himself back on the right side of the looking glass.

Chapter 10

The doorbell rang, rousing both Dick and Diane from their deep slumber. *Oh, Lord!* Dick thought, as he grabbed his bathrobe and rushed down the stairs for the door. *Something pretty bad must have happened to someone – somewhere – for them to come to the parsonage at this hour.* Dick secured the robe and opened the door. There was Leonard, standing on the porch with his usual big smile. Dick mentally struggled to make sense of what he was seeing, and finally blurted out: "Oh, Leonard! One of us has made a terrible mistake!"

"My bet is on you, Dick." Leonard said with a laugh. "It's five after seven. I was running a bit late, myself." Diane heard Leonard's voice and had looked at the clock. Somehow they both forgot to set it. It had been a late night. After the youth group meeting everyone had wanted to play one last board game, so they all had stayed up past their normal bedtimes. *No time for breakfast,* she thought. *I'll pack an egg sandwich for him, then wake the girls. He's going to have to find his coffee somewhere along the route.* She passed Dick who was bounding up the stairs, as she hurried down the stairs for the kitchen. Leonard strolled in and found a seat at the kitchen table. "No need to rush yourself, Diane. We always allow some extra time in case something goes wrong. This is just one of those cases."

Diane smiled at him in response, but kept spreading mayonnaise on the bread as if she were in some speed contest. She appreciated Leonard and understood why Dick was so fond of him. Kind, steady, wise, practical – a simple, straight-forward person. "What you see is what you get with Leonard," Dick had told her, and the years had affirmed those words. Dick once told her how Leonard's pessimistic roommate had spent most of the first evening of a semester determining how much reading would be required of them, how much time they would have to read, and then announced to Leonard that the task was impossible. Leonard had merely looked up from his book, smiled and replied, "Maybe so, but while you were figuring that out I read eighty-two pages."

Dick rushed in, assured Diane that he had awakened and said goodbye to the girls, grabbed the sandwich as he gave her a quick hug and kiss, and followed Leonard out the door. Diane watched, gently rubbing her cheeks: *Dick forgot to shave again,* she mused. Since it was Leonard's turn to drive, he had his Buick. It was large, roomy and fast. They sped off into the darkness like the Green hornet's Black Beauty, heading in search of adventure. Once they had traversed the back roads and were on old 12, Leonard spoke: "I had one of those 'gottcha' experiences this weekend, Dick. You know the neighboring farmer I told you about – the one who has no use for God or the church." Dick nodded. "Well a while back he had asked me why I would leave farming to go back to school to become a preacher man. I told him that God had called me, and he had said, 'God? God? I've been farming this land for forty years and I've never seen no God – much less talked with him.'" He paused to let this point register. Then continued: "Saturday, I was out by the barn, putting some things in order when he came up to me holding a shoebox in his hands, like it was a case holding the crown jewels. I looked in and there was this batch of arrowheads – about twenty or more. I asked him where he had found them. 'Lying in my field,' he replied. 'Didn't you ever see any of these around your place?' he asked me. 'Never did,' I admitted. He smiled that smart aleck smile he sometimes uses and said, 'You've got to think *arrowheads*. That's the only way to find them. *Think arrowheads.* I go out in the fields thinking arrowheads. That's why I see them and others don't.'   Frankly, Dick, I was getting tired of this guy's superior attitude. He doesn't need the church. He doesn't need God. He's so sure that he's smarter than everybody else. Then it dawned on me what to say – or maybe . . ." he said this with a glance upward, "it was given to me to say, 'John, you think arrowheads when you're in the field. That's why you find these little stone trinkets. I think *God.* Maybe that's why I see Him and you don't.'"

"What did he say to that?"

"Nothing. His face fell and he turned and walked off. It was a gottcha moment." He chuckled again when he recalled the moment. Then he turned to Dick and said, more seriously, "Dick, when you're studying your theology and history – and reading the New Testament in Greek – what are you thinking?" Then, as though to emphasize his point, he rephrased his question: "What are you looking for?" Dick winced inside. *Maybe,* he thought, *this is another of those gottcha moments.* Leonard continued, "You spend a lot of time in your head, Dick. We all admire that. You're going to walk away from here with a better education and much higher grades than most of us. But you do spend a great deal of time tending to your head. Are you spending enough time on your soul?"

"Plato believed that the mind shaped the soul, Leonard. You cannot believe what your mind does not understand. I'm after the intellectual framework. That's what seminary is about."

Leonard smiled, "Okay, Dick. Think theology. Think history."

They both settled into silence; Leonard reflecting upon his victory. Dick reflecting upon Leonard's words. *There's no doubt that logic is not helping me with Irene's visitor.*

Perhaps it is time to search elsewhere for answers. "God is spirit and those who worship Him must worship him in spirit and in truth." That's what Jesus told the lady at the well in John 4. So how does one worship in spirit – pneuma? Is it a mood – a frame of mind – another realm of being and thinking? Perhaps seminary should offer a basic course: Spirit 101.

They continued driving in silence, picking up Bob, then Ken, and finally Ron. With Ron aboard, Dick asked, "We've got a light week ahead, fellas. How about taking some time on Wednesday evening to have a God Makers seminar – in my room.?" This seemed satisfactory to everyone. It would be an interesting break from the routine. Wednesday was curried chicken night at the dining hall. They had long-since tired of that and agreed to eat elsewhere, so they could just eat out and move the party to Dick's room. Dick used the driving time to catch up on his interrupted sleep. He awoke for a moment as they passed an Arbys. *Another hour and twenty minutes to go*, he thought and closed his eyes once more.

CHAPTER 11

Dick's room was on the third floor of the old dorm. There were only two other rooms on the floor and that is why Dick had selected it. They crowded into the room and sat on the bed facing blank newsprint which Dick had taped on the wall. "Lecture time?" Ken inquired. "Not at all," Dick assured him. "This is just to let us see what we know." "Okay, " asked Bob, "What do we know?"

"First let's agree what we want to know – to explore." There were nods in general agreement, so Dick continued. " Scripture, Tradition, Experience, and Reason. Sound familiar?"

"That's Wesley's quadrilateral for doing theology," offered Ron proudly.

"Good! So let's follow it for an overview of what we do know – and do not know but might believe we do." Bob and Ken moved forward on the bed. This was going to be fun. "Let's look first at Scripture. This is our rule and guide. Some people believe it is the divinely inspired word of God. Some believe it is the actual dictated Word of God – though how they believe that is beyond me. They use some system of logic that is totally foreign to me, and when I encounter someone of this persuasion we just have to agree to disagree."

"I want to look at the Synoptics first. We have pretty good evidence that Mark is the oldest. Right? The testimony of Papias, bishop of Hieropolis is as close as we can come to verification of any of the authorships. He said that Mark was the recorder for Simon Peter and wrote down all he could remember, but not in chronological order. Since Matthew and Luke both follow the chronology of Mark we assume they had copies in front of them as they wrote. We know a lot about Simon Peter because Mark was his memoirs. We know nothing of Matthew and Luke because they were not in the stories told. John came much later. By this time Christology had developed so that Jesus was no longer a spirit-filled person as in Mark, but was actually an aspect of God: the divine Logos. People play a lot of mental gymnastics to make these fit, but I prefer Ockham's Razor."

"The simplest explanation is the best – or at least the first one to work with," put in Bob – with his personal annotations.

"Right! Also remember the functional definition of truth?"

"The hypothesis which satisfactorily answers every question," responded Bob, quickly.

"Right, again! So give me a simple working hypothesis for this, will you: The Synoptics set the date of the Last Supper at Passover (sometimes called the Feast of Unleavened Bread) and have Jesus serving 'artos – Greek for leavened bread – not azumos or unleavened bread. Then he is crucified on the next day, which - since Jews began their day at sundown – would still be the Passover. John, on the other hand says the Last Supper was two days before the Passover, and says that Jesus has to be removed from the cross before sundown, because that would begin the Day of Preparation. If Jesus could not be on the cross on the day of Preparation – a relatively minor holy day – how come he could be crucified on the Passover itself?"

No one said a word. Finally Ken spoke: "That kind of kicks Biblical Inerrancy in the groin, doesn't it?"

"One of these Gospels has to be wrong," added Bob. Even Ron nodded agreement.

"I've heard that the Passover was celebrated on a different day in Galilee, and that this is what Jesus and the disciples were doing," offered Leonard.

"I've heard that, too, but there is absolutely no proof of that. It's just a pious attempt to make these stories fit." Dick waited. Then he added "Now comes the sticker: Tell me why anyone believes that Revelation was written by the same person who wrote John. Both were written around the beginning of the second century, so there had been plenty of time to think through the meaning of Jesus' life, yet not much time for a person to radically change that understanding in the brief time between the times these two books were written."

"Say that again in English, Dick." Leonard wanted Dick to declare and define himself. In the carpool discussions he was too agile at slipping out of an illogical corner by redefining himself as he went.

"Okay, simply put, we allow seventy or more years for the writer or writers to formulate their theology and Christology. It should be pretty well embedded in their minds. How then in the course of ten or so years do we find such a difference if both were written by the same person?"

"The Gospel of John and the letters written by the same author told of a loving, redeeming deity. Revelation depicts a deity who is just short of a vengeful maniac."

If anyone believes that the events he predicts are still going to happen, we live in a world containing billions of people, and this loving God depicted as a forgiving Father by Jesus is going to slay and condemn all but one hundred and forty-four thousand?" He paused to let the magnitude of the event register. "To push this in another direction: the author of Revelation identifies himself as John of Patmos and claims to be a prophet to give his words some authority. If he were the disciple mentioned in Scripture he would have done better to call himself an Apostle, which carried much more weight with the early church. Further, that apostle was known as John of Ephesus – not Patmos. You can go to Ephesus today and see a replica of the home where tradition claims he lived with Mary, Jesus' mother."

"We have a huge group of 'Christians' who glean all their beliefs from Revelation and Daniel, running around like Henny Penny, knocking on doors saying 'The sky is falling,' trying to talk people into becoming one of those lucky 144,000. We know that Jewish Rabbis laugh at us for having put the Book of Daniel among the prophets. They have it listed among the later writings and know it is historical fiction." Again, he paused to give the group time to digest this.

"Yet, all of these people are well-intentioned, sincere, loving people who genuinely believe they are doing God's will as they pound on doors and give their message."

"So, what's your point?" asked Bob.

"What makes us think we have a better grip on God than they have? From our perspective they are really off-track. From theirs, it is we who are to be pitied for our ignorance. What makes us right? What makes us so certain we are right when we tell our congregations what God is like and God expects of us?"

"Everyone one of us has our special canon – our tiny, personal collection from Scripture which we use to define God – and Jesus – and Spirit." Dick smiled as Bob said this. Bob was observant – very observant. He noticed things. He saw things as they were. That had served him well when he was an astronomer, tracking satellites for NASA. It served him well in this pursuit of understanding God.

"If we didn't we'd have a jumble of contradictions, and never a clear image of the God of Jesus Christ," Ken threw in.

"So we pick and choose to shape the image that goes with our experience and reason. Some focus on punishment. Some on grace and forgiveness. Others create little formulae for simple minds. And still others give gentle directions and encouragement for working out one's own salvation 'in fear and in trembling' as Paul wrote. Right?"

"Okay, Dick. This is what you meant by saying we are the God Makers. You make a good case, but what's the alternative and what do we do about it?" Leonard, with his practical mind wanted to cut to the chase.

"Not so fast, Leonard. We still have to look at Tradition."

"This is enough for me, tonight. Dick" Leonard rose to leave. "I want to think on this for a while, and I still need to do some reading to stay on schedule."

The others rose and left with Leonard. Dick sat back in his chair, and his thoughts drifted back to Napoleon and the unwanted guest of Irene's. *I wish I was as sure –*

or even – had a hint – of what in God's name is happening there. "God's name!" It had been a while since he had used that term outside of the pulpit. *Maybe Leonard was on to something,* he silently admitted. *Maybe I've been attempting to give answers that have no answers – at least none that we can demonstrate by logical syllogisms.* He reflected on this for a while.

Since Thomas Aquinas, the great, medieval Scholastic theologian finally deduced that the "Holy Spirit remains a holy mystery," perhaps I need to locate a means to enter that mystery. Otherwise I'm just a person watching from the outside in. He reflected on this for a moment. *I guess it's time I got to know Irene's guest.*

The thought of this sent chills running through his body, but also created a sense of peace. At least some new direction was taking shape. He rose from his chair, looked around the room at his collection of books and notebooks. Then he settled himself back in his chair. *I suppose now is a good time to work at the other end, as well.* He breathed a sigh; closed his eyes; steadied his breathing and began to enter into a practice he had misplaced along the way. He began to meditate – silently – allowing his consciousness to drift away from the present surroundings – resting himself – his soul – in what Paul once called the One "in whom we live and move . . . and have our being." He began to whisper the mantra he had composed for this exercise of settling himself in that which Paul Tillich called "The Ground of Being." "Aionion Cheiroi . . . Aionion Cheiroi . . ." This was Greek for *everlasting hands.* He watched his stray thoughts and symbols float by with the same detachment he had as a child, when he would lie on a hillside on a summer's day, and watch the clouds – and an occasional bird drift by, feeling himself nestled into the landscape . . . feeling himself as one with the entire universe . . . safely resting in the hands of God.

Chapter 12

As they bundled themselves into Leonard's Buick, Ron suggested the shore route home. "Less traffic and straighter route . . . and we can pick up a gyros and Pepsi on the way." Nobody argued so Leonard headed due south on Sheridan road, passing the Pregnant Pig on the way.

"What a name for a library!. St George certainly has a way with words." Ken still enjoyed chuckling over this seminary joke.

Dick picked up on that and added, "Dr. Buttrick does have a way with more than words. We all know the joke about the student who asked why Buttrick looked out that stained glass window and returned with gems, while he looked and returned with junk. 'Maybe you don't see what Dr. Buttrick sees,' was the professor's reply." Even as he said that, Dick inwardly winced, for he was reminded of Leonard's story about thinking - then seeing - either God or arrowheads.

Leonard, perhaps sensing this, threw in, "What is it that St. George sees that most of us do not?"

Ken responded, "Do you recall the story I'm sure he tells in every introductory preaching class? How the kindly old preacher brought him a book of sermon outlines and a book of illustrations? He said he thanked the preacher. The preacher then left, believing he had helped out the budding, young preacher . Then Buttrick said he stared at the books for a few minutes, then picked them up and deposited them in the waste basket. He said that decision was the most important he ever made in his ministry. Picture what would have happened had Buttrick kept and used those books. One of the world's greatest preachers would have been just another hack."

"So what does Buttrick see?" asked Ron, as though on cue. Ken shook his head and replied, "Whatever it is, it is real – not something he read about or heard about – but something he lived and believed."

"Did you ever go into a Cokesbury book store at the start of a new year?" Bob asked rhetorically, knowing they all had at one time or another. "The Minister's Annuals are stacked up waist high. They must sell hundreds of them: Sermons for every Sunday . . . including Mothers Day."

"And there are tons of books offering lively and timely illustrations for every occasions," added Ken. "Every preacher tells them like they happened to him."

"And they all have the odor of plastic to them," said Dick with disdain.

"Don't be so hard on these guys. A lot of preachers find it hard to come up with sermon ideas Sunday after Sunday." Leonard was playing the good guy. Everyone there knew he never drew from prepackaged sermon material.

"Why, then, do they believe they have a divine call to proclaim the gospel?" This was a topic Dick had wrestled with many times when he encountered some of the poor and plasticized preaching in his travels. "Perhaps God should have just called them to peddle the books of sermons they copy so regularly. They have nothing to proclaim, and they know it. Deep down inside, they have to know it."

"Okay, Okay. Let's get back on the subject." Leonard was the peace maker, the one who could calm troubled waters. "What is it that Dr. Buttrick sees – or knows – that causes him to preach with such power? That's what we all would like to know."

"Simply put," Dick replied, "I believe the man has a pastor's heart. You know that his classes seem to teach as much about pastoral care as about preaching. I believe he has lived out the loving and grace proclaimed by Jesus so fully that it is second nature to him. He's allowed himself to be drawn into that realm of God wherein he lives in some mystical fellowship." Dick surprised himself with these words. He knew them to be true, but he did not quite understand how he knew them to say them.

"Dick," said Leonard quietly, so that only the two of them heard the words, "I believe you may have begun to *think* God."

He said nothing. Thursday evening he had repeated the practice of meditation; this time for an hour. In the classes on Thursday and Friday morning, he had found himself paying less attention to memorizing the lectures and more intent on digging beneath the words to understand what the teachers – even the ordinary teachers - were saying about their faith.

Dick noticed the dilapidated brake relining shop that sat by itself in a wooded area, and quietly calculated, *Hmm, fifty seven minutes - closer to home than I thought.*

CHAPTER 13

Dick decided to just drop by Irene's without calling beforehand. Something was always happening. He might as well go and see. This time, before he left his car he paused and offered a silent prayer – for Irene and for whatever it was that was upsetting her. He prayed for himself, as well, that he might be more open to whatever was happening and be used as an instrument for healing.

"Make me an instrument of your peace," he thought. *St. Francis had the right idea. Get the ego out of the way . . . and let the true self emerge.* Dick found himself thinking in Jungian terms. The *Self* or *Imago Dei*, as Carl Jung described it is the true, deeper self which lies beneath our consciousness. The goal in life is to allow the superficial self – the ego – to dissolve into the Self. He sat there for another minute, putting those thoughts to rest, although planning to return to them later, but for the moment, trying to recapture the mood of prayer. He definitely would require help from someone – somewhere - with this unwanted visitor of Irene's.

"Pastor Dick?" Irene was surprised by Dick's unannounced visit. It had taken her a couple of minutes to answer the door, and Dick hoped he had not interrupted some family or personal business.

"I was in the neighborhood, so I thought I'd just drop by to see how things were going," he lied. "Has everything been quiet, or has something happened that I should know?" *Although I don't have the slightest idea what I would do if something has happened,* he acknowledged to himself. He was starting to feel like some quack – a pretender – no matter how well-intentioned he was.

Irene hesitated for just a moment, then offered, "We were just using the ouija board. Would you like to come in and see how it works?"

Dick nodded and began to follow Irene into another room. He wondered if Walter was working the board with her. It seemed to have scared off all the neighbors. However, when he entered the room he was startled to see little Danny sitting at the table.

"We just started to use it when you arrived," she explained. "This will show you how it works." Irene sat down opposite Danny, put her hands on the marker. "Who are you?" she asked. Then waited. It did not take long before the marker began to spell a word: "m-o-t-h-e-r." Dick had been watching carefully to see if either one of them seemed to be moving the marker. Both had held it lightly, however. If either was causing this, it was subtle.

"Why are you here?" Irene asked. Again there was a brief pause and the marker began to move" "l-o-v-e" it spelled. "What do you mean, 'love?'" Irene said insistently. "l-o-v-e" the board repeated. Irene looked at Dick in exasperation, "That's all it ever says!" "Why are you here? What do you want? What does it mean? 'Love – love – love' – that's all it will say."

She thought for a minute, then asked a different question: "How long do you intend to stay here?" The wait this time seemed interminable. Dick wondered if Danny was trying to think of something he could spell, or if – just possibly – whatever , or whoever was causing that marker to move needed to think about the answer.

Dick's first thought was, *Danny doesn't know how to spell many words. He's only five.* He decided to intervene to see just who was controlling the marker.

"Will you speak to me?" he asked gently.

The movement of marker was almost violent: "No!" It seemed to shout the answer.

"Why not?" asked Dick, thinking this would be the tip off as to who was making that marker go.

"Skeptic!" Again the marker seemed to rush madly to spell out its answer.

"You're right! I am a skeptic, and I don't believe in you. I don't believe in you at all." Dick was now caught up in the game – or whatever it was that was being played. Danny didn't know words like "skeptic." If Irene was doing this she had some kind of emotional problem that ran pretty deep. This was the time to find out. *Push her*, he thought. *Push her till something gives.*

"You can't even answer a civil question. Any host has the right to ask a guest when they intend to leave. And don't give me that 'I'm her mother' bit. Any respectable guest will tell their host how long they intend to stay under their roof. Come on! What's your answer?"

Finally, after what seemed like a long wait for an elevator, the marker began to move: "C-h-r-i-s-t-m-a-s." "You will go home after Christmas?" Irene asked urgently. "Y-e-s---a-f-t-e-r—C-h-r-i-s-t-m-a-s" the board responded. Irene looked at Dick with relief. "That's just three weeks from now."

Suddenly the marker moved again. This time it spelled a word that one does not use in polite company. "What!"

shouted Irene. *I didn't know Danny knew words like that*, thought Dick. In response, the board spelled another, even less-acceptable word. "Mother, what are you doing?" shouted Irene again. Again the board spelled out a four letter word one just never uses except in pornographic literature. "Pastor Dick, Make her stop."

This either had to be Danny's doings, or Irene was releasing some deep-seated frustrations. "Tell your mother that if she swears again you will put away the board and never talk with her again." Dick spoke this as an order. Not to be discussed – only obeyed. Irene addressed the board and said, "Mother if you ever use that kind of language again I will *throw* this board away, and never speak to you again. *Do you understand?*"

The marker's response was slow and measured. It was easy to imagine the writer with head down and an apologetic look on her face: "Yes" was the simple response.

"Tell her again, just to be certain she understands that you are serious about this."

Irene repeated her threat and the board repeated its response.

Good, Dick thought. *Whatever is going on here will stop. Irene has enough problems without adding a foul-mouthed marker.* The thought almost made him laugh, but there was something about this that did not evoke laughter.

That seemed to be enough for the day. For the first time, Dick felt as though he might actually have helped out – though he had no idea how that might have been.

"I'll let myself out, Irene. Danny take good care of your mother. She is a special lady and she loves you very much." He threw that in just in case Danny had any ideas of continuing to play whatever tricks he might be . . . playing?

Back in the car, he paused to say a word of prayer and to steady himself. He felt as though he had been in some kind of contest. Dick rarely ever sweated, but he could feel the wetness under his arms as he started his drive home.

CHAPTER 14

"Anyone have a Bible?" The rest of the weekend had gone smoothly. Dick was ready to pick up the God Makers discussion, but had waited until Ron was safely tucked into a rear seat before starting. Since many of their discussions concerned Scripture or sermons, Dick was certain there would be some Bibles in the group. "Just might have one or two of those things back here in the amen corner," answered Bob. Ken was driving today, so he would have to keep most of his mind directed on the traffic. It was understood that safety was the primary factor for whoever was driving. They passed too many home-made cross markers along the highway not to be aware that carelessness could be fatal.

"Someone turn to Mark 8:27."

"I've got it!" Ron answered.

"Good. Now someone else find Matthew 16:13 and also Luke 9: 18."

"I'll get them," said Leonard.

"Today, we look at Tradition. Let's see how some of these teachings of the church got started, and if they still do – or ever did – make sense. When Jesus asks the disciples who people say he is, Peter gives his answer. Ron, what does Peter say in Mark?"

"You are the Christ."

"Nothing more?"

"No. Nothing, just 'You are the Christ'."

"What's Jesus' reaction?"

"He commands them not to tell anyone."

"That's all?"

"That's all."

"Leonard, you have Luke. What does he have Peter say?"

"Basically the same thing: 'You are the Christ of God.'"

"What's Jesus' response?"

"The same as in Mark: 'Don't' tell anyone.'"

"Now read Matthew's version of Peter's answer and Jesus' response. What's different?"

"Peter adds, 'The son of the Living God,' to 'You are the Christ,' and Jesus' response is, 'Blessed are you, Simon Bar-Jona! For flesh and blood has not revealed this to you but my Father who is in heaven. And I tell you, you are Peter, and on this rock I will build my church and the powers of death shall not prevail against it. I will give you the keys of the kingdom of heaven, and whatever you bind on earth shall be bound in heaven, and whatever you loose on earth shall be loosed in heaven. Then he gave his disciples strict orders not to tell anyone.'"

"Did anyone notice a difference?" Dick inquired rhetorically. Then he immediately continued: "Since Mark is accepted as the memoirs of Peter wouldn't you think that Peter might have remembered that event? It is an obvious gloss – or later addition to the text."

He paused for a moment, then went on: "Matthew has many glosses which show some later development of the thinking around Christ and the role of the Church. Remember, the canon wasn't established until late in the 4th century. The church was sorting through all the writings to see what they considered being worthy of instruction. Since no copyrights were available, the writings were fair game for any scribe who thought he had a better understanding."

"We know that the first two major Christian centers were Antioch and Alexandria. Rome only rose to prominence later. The church at Antioch was known to have been founded by the refugees from Jerusalem when it fell in 70 A.D.. The church at Alexandria claimed to have been founded by Mark. When Rome rose to prominence, it claimed Peter as its founder. Since Peter had been martyred there, he was the natural choice. The problem is that – aside from what the Roman Catholic Church claims - there is no evidence that Peter ever was its first bishop. Actually there is more circumstantial evidence that he was not."

"How do you figure that?" put in Ken, who was paying attention even if not free to do the mental wrestling.

"First, the early leaders of the church in Rome were called presiders or presidents – not bishops. I know that's picky, but stay with me. The claim made by the church is that Peter was placed in charge of it by Jesus. Anyone with half a mind knows that James, Jesus' brother, was the head of the church in Jerusalem. That was the original church. Read Acts carefully and you know James was the top man. Peter changed his behavior when James' men came to visit him and Paul. This is not the action of someone who was *in charge*. I saved the best argument for last, however: Read the final chapter of Romans, chapter 16. Paul sent greeting to everyone there whom he knew . . . but he never mentioned Simon Peter!" He paused now to let the significance of that register.

"Doesn't that seem a bit strange to you? If Peter was believed to be there as head of the church, and Paul never even gives him a nod, should that not raise flags for any respectable Biblical theologian?"

"How about the church's claim that Jesus made Peter head of the church at the morning fish fry reported in John 21?"

"Good question, Leonard. Glad you asked it, or I would have forgotten and left this hanging. You all remember that Peter denied Jesus three times after he had proclaimed he never would do that. Picture this then: Peter realizes it is Jesus standing on the shore and he jumps into the water to rush to him. Then – as he is about to greet him – he recalls his bold vow and his cowardly denial, and stands there ashamed. I imagine him lurking in the morning shadows – too embarrassed to enter into the celebration that is going on. After breakfast, Jesus puts his arm around Simon Peter and leads him away from the group."

"Now let me go back to an earlier story, the one of Jesus praying in Gethsemane. There he prayed for God to 'remove this cup.' Every time he returned to check on Peter, James and John, how did he find them?"

"They were asleep," said Ron.

"Right, so since Jesus was arrested there and never got the opportunity to speak to any of the disciples again, how do we know what Jesus prayed about in the garden that night?'

Dick did not give them time to respond, but answered his own question:

"I think that he told it to Peter as they walked that morning after the fish-fry. Incidentally, this – to me – is another proof of the resurrection. How else could anyone know the story? Anyway, I picture Jesus saying to Peter, 'I understand how you felt. It was all I could do to keep from walking up to Bethany and heading back to Galilee.' Then he told him of his own struggle in prayer."

"So, how does that fit in with your point?" asked Ken.

"I guess I got sidetracked. Okay, it is this: Peter denied Jesus three times. Jesus has him affirm his love and loyalty three times. Jesus asks Peter, 'Do you love me?' and three times Peter says, 'Yes.' Peter is emotionally reinstated. It's that simple."

"How come no one else has ever taught or written this, Dick?"

"I have no idea, Bob. Someone probably wrote it, but it got lost along the way. I just know that it seemed so transparently clear when I began to reflect on it that I would gladly debate the issue with anyone who wished to dispute this theory. If I was a lawyer and Peter was accused of being the first head of the church, I know I could get him off."

"So Peter might not have been the first Pope. What does that have to do with us Protestants?"

"Good point, Ron. It was the church which was centered in Rome which developed some of the early doctrines that still cling to us. If they have no special authority except the innate authority of being true and relevant then it behooves us to see whether they are, in fact, true and relevant. Right?"

"Hey, can we hold off on this stuff until I can get into the discussion, too?" Ken asked.

"Okay. We'll wait until no one is driving and give us all a clear shot at it." With this, the group settled back into their customary routines. Ron curled over for a quick nap. Leonard set up his chess board and invited Bob to play. Ken began humming an oldie, "When you're a long, long way from home," and Dick settled back and decided to try a few moments of quiet meditation. As he was about to close his eyes, he observed the now-empty frozen custard stand along side of the road, just past the also-closed drive-in theater. *An hour and ten minutes to go. More time than I need.*

He closed his eyes, steadied his breathing, and with the soft melody being hummed by Ken faintly drifting through his consciousness, he began his soundless mantra, *Aionion Keiroi . . . Aionion Keiroi . . .* and slowly faded from the confines of the car.

CHAPTER 15

The week had been filled with papers due (and overdue for some) and preparation for finals. There had been no time for the God Makers Seminar, as it was now called. The ride home was used to prepare sermons and lessons for the weekend work bee. The darkness hit them when they were only half way home. Each knew it was only a matter of weeks before the snow would arrive and turn the highways into slippery roller coasters that caused those little home made crosses to appear in the medians and shoulders. That, in itself, sobered the mood, and transformed the eastward trip into more of an endurance contest than an anticipated homecoming. There had been no singing, no jokes - not even any small talk. Weary and worn might have been the proper adjectives to describe this crew of students-pastors-husbands-fathers rolled into one.

The Friday evening ritual was reenacted: First Debbie, but this time Dick held her a bit longer. She had been born when he was in Korea and he had not seen her until she was nine months old. Now, here he was: an absentee father once more. She was growing up too quickly and he was missing some of the best parts. "I love you," he whispered in her ear." She knew that, of course. Still, it was pleasant to hear and pleasant to say. He turned to Diane: "Home is the sailor; home from the sea, and the hunter home from the hill." She nodded, reading his weariness in his posture and in his eyes. They exchanged a simple hug – a gentle kiss. They had touched again. He was home . . . for a while, at least. Dick turned toward the back room; gave a sigh and slowly entered the semi-darkness Cindy used for privacy. He knelt down by her and stroked her hair. Then he gently lifted her and placed her on his knee. She cuddled closer, then looked up and gave him a big smile, seeming to realize that this time it was Daddy who needed to be comforted. *Another year and a half – less even. This rat race will be over, and we can live like a normal family again.* The thought lightened the moment and he arose with a smile. "What's for supper?" he asked.

At exactly eight o'clock the telephone rang. *That has to be Irene*, Dick thought as he groped for the phone. *She must have been waiting for what seemed a reasonable time.*

He cleared his throat, forced a smile which would be reflected in his voice and offered a cheery, "Good Morning! This is the Methodist parsonage. Can I be of service?"

"Pastor Dick?" Sure enough it was Irene's voice.

"Yes, Irene. What's happening?" Dick had learned to ask that very general question which then could elicit any number of responses. It worked much better than. "How are you?" That almost always evoked, "Fine," as a response, and he had to start anew to learn the reason for a call.

"Something new has happened, and this is rather upsetting. Can you come over?"

"I've some things I need to take care of here, Irene." *A shave and a shower, dressing, breakfast . . . just a few little things,* He mentally ticked off the routine. "How does nine o'clock sound?" Dick had learned that Irene would accept any time he offered, so he saw no reason to rush.

Dick headed his car to Irene's, pulled up to the curb, stepped out of the car, and took a quick look around. He knew that Major was safe in the day time, but still . . . he liked to know he was not being stalked. Then he walked to the door, and knocked.

"Come in and sit down, Pastor Dick." No niceties this time. Right down to business! *Something is really different*, he realized, as he settled himself into an overstuffed chair in the living room. Dick started to lean back, then decided he looked more earnest – more intent – if he leaned forward so that's what he did.

"The light!" She exclaimed. "Now it's the light!" With this, she tightened her lips and just stared at Dick for a moment. "We've got a light in the closet. It looks a lot like that small light that we saw in our bedroom with Danny. But now it's in the closet!"

"Is it there now?" Dick inquired, half hoping she would say no, and half hoping she would say yes, so he could see it for himself.

"No, it only showed up on Monday, Wednesday, and Friday. And then, only late at night. I happened to see it when Walter came home late and I offered to put his coat away. There it was: Big as life. Just hanging in mid air, shining away like it belonged there."

"Does it do anything but shine?" Dick asked weakly, trying to make some sense of what Irene was saying.

"No it just hangs there and shines." Dick felt a wave of relief pass over him. "At least it's not doing any damage," he mused. He was tempted to suggest that if it was not hurting anything she just keep the closet door closed and forget about it, like one would ignore an occasional burst of static on the radio. He realized as quickly as the thought arose, that this would brand him as completely inept at this ghost busting business.

He was at a loss. He decided to fake it, so he arose and asked, "Where is the closet""

"Right by the front door."

He strode over to the front door, trying to give an imitation of a television detective looking for clues. He opened the closet door, peered inside, uttered a "hmmm," and returned to Irene, as confused as to what to say or do as when he began this charade.

"Irene, there is nothing I can do, since the light is not there, and since it is neither threatening or harming anyone, let's just watch and see what happens." He said this as a doctor might who had made a thorough diagnosis and now was writing the prescription. Irene seemed to accept this, and nodded her agreement.

"If anything threatening happens – anything at all. Do not wait until next Saturday. Call me at the seminary. Here's my number." *If all I can give is some sense of comfort and assurance, I certainly can do that,* he decided, as he looked about for Major and returned to his car. Before starting the car, he paused to reflect upon all the events which had taken place in that house:

Footsteps across the living room floor.

Danny claiming Irene's mother was his friend.

Tipped over pictures.

Minnie locked out and scared out of her wits.

A light that jumped from wall to wall and seemed to call Danny.

An open specimen bottle lifts itself up, makes a Ferris wheel arc and lands without spilling a drop.

An ouija board that frightened away neighbors, but told of things unknowable to them.

The table board in the baby's crib.

The same ouija board that identified its mover as Mother, acting out of love, and promised to go home after Christmas.

A swearing ouija board that used words Danny could not have known or spelled.

Now this light – back, and hanging out in the closet every other night.

No clue! None at all. Dick was about ready to admit that what was in that house escaped all logic and could only be explained – or known – if one was willing to step outside the normal parameters that define reality.

On the way back home, the thought occurred to him, *If Irene does call, what will I do then?* He shrugged, shook his head, and increased his speed, as if to rush back to the safety and comfort of the other side of the looking glass.

CHAPTER 16

Once Ron was comfortably settled in his favorite nook in the back seat, Dick reconvened the God Makers seminar. "The church in Jerusalem celebrated Christus Victor: The victorious Christ, Jesus of Nazareth had met death head on, and had overcome it. Charles Wesley says it in his hymn, 'Christ the Lord is Risen Today': '*Death in vain forbids him rise.*' The ancients had a totally different way of looking at life. They understood curses and hexes. They dwelt in a world filled with demons. Death, or Thanatos, was a force that claimed souls and brought them to his private domain. Jesus allowed Death to believe he was a mere human, so Thanatos fell into his trap. Once Jesus was raised, Death lost his power over humanity. Never again could he hold them. When Jerusalem fell and the church fled to Antioch, their leaders taught that Jesus, the Son-of-Man or Second Adam, had come to undo the failure of Adam, the First Man. He was obedient, even to the death, so God raised him to eternal life, as Adam would have had eternal life if he had behaved himself. We who follow must emulate Jesus in faithfulness so that we, too, will be raised from the dead into eternal life. Unfortunately, Antioch faded and Rome rose to prominence, so we inherited their rather legalistic understanding of the work of Christ. It's just as well, though. The Antioch doctrine may have made sense for the people of the 1ˢᵗ century, but it sounds like mere superstition now."

"Okay, Dick," said Ken, "The early church is your specialty. Most of us just get a smattering – and overview of that era. Tell us more of what you know."

Dick grinned. "The two earliest centers of Christianity were Antioch and Alexandria. One was Jewish in its orientation. The other was Greek. Their world views were very different, so their interpretation of the work of Jesus also was different."

"Antioch was Jewish in its understanding: Micah's, '*You know, O man, what God requires of you: Do justly, love mercy, and walk humbly with your God.*' The Christian life was simple. Follow the teachings of the Torah. Treat others with respect. Genuinely care for them. Maintain your awareness of God's Presence in your life. Then relax, and do not worry about what follows this life. God will provide as God has always provided. In spite of the quaintness of the theology I like the conclusion. It's straight forward."

"Too bad we didn't stick with that," put in Leonard. "I could have kept on farming, and just done some part-time teaching."

"I could have stayed with NASA, tracking satellites," added Bob.

"You're probably right. I don't think Jesus planned on starting a church. He was proclaiming a whole new way of living and viewing the world. Let's take a look at what happened outside of Judaism: The Eastern Church, centered in Alexandria, viewed the world through Plato's structure. Their doctrine of salvation was also straight forward. 'The Divine became human so that the human could become divine.' They had no doctrine of atonement. Their perception of God did not require one. Obedience to Jesus' teachings coupled with participation in holy communion, 'The medicine of our immortality,' as Polycarp called it, was all that was required.. We were made in God's image. We had the potential to become divine."

"Polycarp was that early martyr who went to Rome and refused to offer a sacrifice to Caesar, isn't he?"

"That's right, Ken. You must have read your assignment that evening. Martyrs had a special authority in the early church once the original apostles had died off. "

"Martyr means 'witness' doesn't it?" Asked Ron.

"Right. They witnessed with their lives, so the early church figured they must have been pretty confident in their faith.. Now, on to our heritage: Rome's world view was more complex. The prevailing philosophy was Stoicism, based on natural law. Also, the social structure was strongly legalistic. Combine these two, and throw in speculative Hellenistic theology, and you get the result we now live with in the Western Church. Guilt and innocence replaced simple grace. The God of Judgment was reinstated and the God of the Prodigal Son parable told by Jesus was shelved.

"The Genesis story claims that we were made in God's image and God breathed life into us. You know that breath and spirit are the same terms in both Hebrew and Greek, so humanity was inspired. The spirit dwells *within* us. Jesus called his listeners 'the light of the world,' and Paul addressed his readers as either 'saints', or 'those called to be saints'. The Western church dubbed us 'sinners'. There is a severe contradiction here, and our forefathers opted for the wrong version."

"The earliest liturgies had only three prescribed prayers: Adoration, Thanksgiving, and Intercession. A fourth, Confession, was added. These followed a prescribed form and emphasized human failings rather than human potential as saints in the making. Luther threw it out of his reformed liturgy, calling it, 'A man-made instrument of the devil,' but he was so addicted to guilt that he quietly reinstated it. Poor guy. He just couldn't feel good unless he felt bad. And, this, my friends, is what we do to the good people who attend our worship and pay our salaries." Dick paused, expecting a strong reaction. He was not to be disappointed.

"Wait a minute!" Ken practically shouted his objection. "Sin is a reality of life. It needs to be dealt with. Jesus' model in what we call 'The Lord's Prayer,' says, 'forgive us our trespasses.' Don't put it all on Luther."

"Good point, Ken. I totally agree with you," said Dick. First, however, let's clarify that trespasses are not the same as sins. Sins are failings. Trespasses are intentional crossings of the boundaries. Trespasses need to be forgiven – by the persons we wrong and by God. Sins – or failings – need correction. The forgiveness for sins needs to come from the persons who suffered from our failures. Jesus assured people that their sins were forgiven by God - even without their asking for it. Loving parents do not condemn their children for their failures. They call them on it but try to help them understand why they failed, but they do not berate them for it. We carry around enough burdens of guilt without being beaten over the head with it. It's the difference in being raised in a home where the parent continually asks,

'Can't you do anything right?' or in a home where the parent says, 'You can do better than that.'"

"Let me address another aspect of our prayers of confession: Asking God for forgiveness when we sin against a neighbor is like asking your parents to forgive you when you've cheated the boy next door. You're talking to the wrong person! You should be asking your neighbor for forgiveness. He is the person you wronged – not God! What we do by this weekly ritual of asking God for forgiveness is to turn God into a divine judge who acts on behalf of all humanity. God forgives and that settles it. No need to do anything else. AA has it right. One of their steps is to ask forgiveness of the person you wronged and attempt to make it right. Asking forgiveness of God without dealing with the person you wronged is a cop out. In his Sermon on the Mount (Matthew 5:23-24) Jesus points that out when he speaks of making your sacrifice at the altar, but first setting things straight with the person you wronged."

"Yeah," whispered Leonard. The others nodded their agreement.

Then Ken spoke up, "How about the sins of omission, when we fail to act to set something right? We've all sat quietly at some time when we should have spoken up for what we believe. We also have had those 'good intentions that the road to Hell is paved with' and then done nothing about them. Don't we need forgiveness for those times? If so, to whom do we turn for that forgiveness?"

"Good point, Ken. I think the Letter of James gives some direction along that line. In 4:17 he writes – and I translate freely from the Greek here because I think it says it more clearly than the English translations I've read: 'Knowing the good to do and not doing it, is a sin – or failure – to himself.' I interpret this to mean that in failing to do the good we fail ourselves – our better selves. To know this and to learn from this is better than trying to receive forgiveness for it. We cannot change the past, but we can learn from the past and resolve not to repeat yesterday's mistakes."

"It seems to me that sins of omission move in two different directions, Dick" said Bob.

"One is not speaking up or acting when we had the chance to set something right. The other is in acting at less than our best when we had the opportunity. There were times we could have been kinder, nicer . . . more attentive or more considerate of others, and we simply chose not to be."

"I think those are the times that still haunt me most." put in Leonard. "Those times when I was too wrapped up in myself to respond to even the simple needs of my family or friends . . . still lay heavily on my soul."

"We've all been there, Leonard. That's what I mean when I say we can't change the past. We can only learn and try not to be so into ourselves in the future. Incidentally," Dick continued, "I address the issue of sins in the time of congregational prayer. I believe that private sharing of our failures with God is important. But it's not to receive forgiveness. Rather, it is in the quiet intimacy of this divine encounter that we can explore our failures honestly, knowing – because Jesus has told us – that God will understand and accept and guide us in what to do. I say something like, 'In the silence let each of us share his or her personal concerns with God. Lift up the good moments and the bad. Ask for understanding of why the bad moments happened – what you might have done differently.' Then let the people dwell on this for a couple of minutes.   There is absolutely no need to rush through prayer - if you are not the one doing all the talking. That gives the people time to commune with God in their own way. The sermon time is the time then to address these failings. Our task is not to lay guilt on people, but to help them to understand their failings and to guide them on their spiritual path. If the people have done their work they will personalize the sermon and think you are a mind reader."

"Okay, I see your point, Dick." Ken said. "General confessions are just that: too general to be of value, except to make someone feel guilty."

Dick nodded, and continued his narrative: "Along came the Reformation and Calvin took control of that (Luther got married and got gout). Calvin elaborated on Paul in a manner that would cause Paul to spin in his grave. *Predestination,* is the term Calvin employed for it. We were either predestined for heaven or for hell. His early theology, of course, was elaborated on and became what we call Calvinism. This God was the God-that-will-get-ya-if-ya-don't-watch-out. The irony, of course, was that since you were predestined, there wasn't much you could do about it. The classic sermon of Puritan America was Jonathan Edward's 'Sinner in the Hands of an Angry God.' How would you like to have lived in those times?"

Ron shuffled nervously, and breathed a "Not really," at this.

"Today," Dick continued, "we have such a variety of deities that no one can make sense of them all. Each of us presents our narrow perspective. We have the God who promises you rewards for good behavior – sort of a 'You scratch my back; I'll scratch yours.' We still have the 'hell fire and damnation God' of Calvinism hanging around. We have the indulgent uncle, who forgives everything as though it does not matter. We have the Social Justice God-of-the-prophets.'"

"What's wrong with that?" Bob asked.

"Not a thing, so long as there is some balance. Some people *only* preach social justice. Some *never* preach it."

"It would upset some of their big givers!" Ken blurted out.

"That, too, I suppose," agreed Dick. "The God of Jesus Christ calls for a balance. 'Love mercy; do justly; walk humbly with your God.' I doubt if any of us ever does more than accidentally stumble onto the correct balance. Scripture doesn't give us enough information. We have to guess – to speculate. Anytime we do that we are saying more about ourselves than about Jesus. Face it!"

"Okay," said Leonard. "Now I understand why you claim we preachers are more in danger of breaking the commandment on not using the Lord's name in vain, than any other breed."

"Right, again, my friend," Dick responded. "Anyone who doesn't enter the pulpit with fear and trembling isn't paying attention to his calling."

With this, the riders settled back into silence. Some reflected on the conversation, weighing its merits and sorting through their personal agendas which have filtered their way into past sermons. Some merely closed their eyes and tried to get a last few minutes of sleep before finals week exploded on them.

Dick fell to musing again. *The reality of a spiritual realm is basic to our faith. I speak of it regularly, so why am I having trouble accepting it? Could it simply be that I heard too many ghost stories as a kid and never really believed them? They were the early sci-fi tales: "The Hermit's Cave" and "Inner Sanctum." They were scary and exciting but not at all believable. Now that I may have one running around the house, I can't accept the possibility that it could be real. John Wesley claimed his father attempted to drive out a disembodied spirit from his attic at Epworth and that it beat the tar out of him. We speak of that as some past curiosity, but never expect to actually experience it ourselves.*

With this he mentally switched subjects and began reviewing class lectures in preparation for the approaching final exams.

CHAPTER 17

Dick took an afternoon break from his studies, and decided to use it for a quick nap. *Fifteen minutes, then wake up*, he told himself. More than that, he had learned, would make him groggy and defeat the purpose of the nap. As he lay on his dorm bed, drifting into the twilight area between waking and sleeping, a vague vision appeared in his mind. He was back at Irene's, staring at the ouija board with Irene on one side and Danny on the other. However, there in the middle was Irene's mother – ghostly in appearance and larger than life. She had one hand placed on Irene's shoulder and the other on Danny's. What was disturbing was that she was staring at Dick, with a satisfied smile.

"I've chased off the others and now I have them both to myself." The words were not spoken. They were merely understood, as though she was able to transplant her thoughts into Dick's consciousness – or what remained of his consciousness.   Startled – Dick awoke and sat straight up.

Good heavens! That's it! He had wondered why the strange actions had occurred around the board, and had never considered that the neighbors were being chased away, so that the only two who remained to work the board were the two persons she cared most about.

What a dream! - - - or I hope it was a dream, Dick thought.   Was it his subconscious working on the problem while he slept?- - or was it - - ? Dick did not even want to consider another possibility. *This is getting to me more than I thought it would – or wanted it to. At least Christmas is coming up in another couple of weeks and then mother dear – or who ever – or whatever it is that is roaming around that house will disappear.* Dick still wanted to believe this was a combination of easily explainable circumstances, but frankly he had run out of explanations. Some subterranean portion of his mind had accepted the fact that a disembodied spirit – probably Irene's mother – had escaped the spiritual realm and invaded the physical world.

Why not? he thought. The spiritual realm gave birth to the physical. Dick believed that and taught about it in his classes at Napoleon. However, it was one thing to t*each* about it. It was quite another *to experience it.* The spiritual realm was some inner domain which he enjoyed delving into through meditation. It was calm – mystical – uniting everything into a wonderful wholeness which caused him to return refreshed, renewed and revitalized.

Dick had read the theories about parallel universes. *Was it possible that one of these is the spiritual, which exists along side the physical in a mode which makes it impossible to experience - - - at least most of the time - - - for most of the people?* Dick mused to himself.

He gave Bob a call and asked him if he had time to take a quick spiritual journey. He knew Bob was a bright student, and did not need to spend every spare moment at the books. He also appreciated his openness of spirit – the cosmopolitan attitude that had developed from his years of traveling the world with NASA. Bob readily agreed, savoring the moment more readily possibly because Dick kept their destination a secret.

They drove northward along Sheridan Road, toward the upper suburbs. The houses became more magnificent as they drove. This definitely was one of the posh suburban areas of Chicago. Eventually they passed into Wilmette, and came to a magnificent structure which looked as though it would feel more at home in India.

"Aaah! The Baha'i Temple," said Bob, immediately recognizing the building. They parked the car and began to circle the building before approaching its entrance.

"Like a miniature Taj Mahal," exclaimed Bob with deep appreciation.

Dick just nodded. He preferred to just bask in the calm serenity the building offered. They found a bench and for a few moments just sat, admiring the simple beauty of its design and construction. Finally, only because they were under some time constraints, they arose and entered the building. Again, they found seats and sat quietly reading the various Scriptures from every great religious tradition which wove their way around the base of the dome.

In differing ways, each was expressing the same belief – the same accepted truth.

The statements in the alcove summed it up:

> *All the prophets of God proclaim the same faith.*
> *So powerful is unity's light that it can illumine the whole earth.*
> *You are the fruits of one tree and the leaves of one branch.*
> *Consort with the followers of all religions with friendliness.*

*O Son of Being! Thou art My lamp and My
light is in thee.
O Son of Being, Walk in My statutes for the
love of Me.
The source of all learning is the knowledge
of God, exalted by His glory.*

Each sat, quietly reading and contemplating the words. Bob had visited many countries that were non-Christian. He had tasted of their philosophies – long before he felt the call to become a proclaimer of Christianity. Dick knew he must be recalling some of those countries and their customs as they sat.

Finally, reluctantly, they arose as if by common consent, and returned quietly to their car. Dick turned the ignition key, felt the kick of the engine. It was at that moment that he was aware, again, of the frigid temperatures. For a moment, all had been calm. All had been . . . well . . . *comfortable*, might be the term.

Bob eventually broke the silence: "We all seek the same God – the same path, you know."

"No doubt about it, and each of us has some kernel of truth we could share. Still . . . .." Dick paused to gather his thoughts. "I look to this man Jesus as the best path I can find. It could be because of my background, but I think he had a better grasp." He paused again. "He lived it!" He hesitated; then continued. "He lived it. He died for his belief and he rose from the dead. That gives him the edge over anyone else. I know the story of *The Bab*, which means the door or gate in Arabic. He was the door for Baha u llah, who founded the Baha'i faith. But, for me, Jesus is that door. He's the Bab or messiah. "

"It works for me," agreed Bob.

"Bob, we live in such an extraordinarily complex mystery, that I don't know how anyone has the arrogance to say that their understanding of the whys and whos is the only one."

Bob just nodded in response, and let Dick continue with his thought.

"I also don't understand why we seem to be afraid to check sources outside our faith to understand what their experience of God is."

"That's easy, Dick. You already answered it. 'Afraid.' The security of a simple belief system which they can accept is preferable to the thought that perhaps – just perhaps – theirs might not be as tight and true as they would like to believe."

"We *are* God Makers, aren't we, Bob? Little God Makers . . . fashioning little, limited gods. In the beginning, God created humanity in his image, and since that time, humanity has been returning the favor."

They drove back into Evanston in silent reflection. The brief trip had carried them further than they had thought – or perhaps – wished – to journey.

CHAPTER 18

Back home again. Diane, Deb, and Cindy beamed at Dick across the dinner table.

"Two weeks!" said Diane.

"Two whole weeks of Daddy," echoed Deb with more than a touch of glee in her voice and eyes.

Cindy just sat quietly and smiled softly – more to herself than to the others – even Dick.

There would be special Christmas Eve services to plan, and some preparations for Watch Night, the church-centered celebration of New Year's Eve for those who wished to usher the year in with prayer rather than alcohol and blaring music. Still, there would be quiet evenings for reaffirming the ties and love that bound them together even when they were separated by too many miles.

There were no phone calls that evening. If anything was happening with Irene's visitor she had learned that it could wait until Saturday morning to be told.

Rather than playing games, the family gathered into the small TV room, and cuddled together, watching inane sitcoms until it was time for the girls to dress for bed. As the girls climbed the stairs, Diane moved close to Dick. *Cuddling has certain advantages over meditation,* Dick thought, as he turned down the sound on the television and allowed the moment to carry itself.

"Time for songs and prayers," the girls chimed in unison, arousing both Diane and Dick from their reverie.

They dutifully scaled the stairs and seated themselves on the girls' beds. Hugs, kisses, a prayer spoken softly, which always served to put the day to rest – wiping away the painful memories of rebukes or other messy moments.

> Father, now the night has come. All my
> work and play are done.
> This has been a happy day ,and now I
> come to Thee and pray.
> Bless the children everywhere. Keep
> them in Thy loving care.
> While we sleep and while we wake, bless
> us all for Jesus' sake. Amen.

"Wagon Wheels, Daddy! Wagon Wheels." It was another ritual. A song passed down from Dick's mother, sung at bedtime. Undoubtedly it would become a ritual for the girls' families – as the evening prayer had been passed along from Diane's family.

There is something very good about family rituals, Dick thought as they descended the stairs and returned to the TV room. This time they did not bother to turn on the set. *They lay claim to some part of our soul that embraces tradition – claiming the past as its ongoing heritage.*

Chapter 19

"Time to visit Irene," Dick said to Diane as he bundled himself into his winter clothing. He had felt it necessary to explain his regular absences to Diane. Confidentiality can still be retained because of the trust he had in her discretion. Many times Dick had heard her response when asked by some curious parishioner about a private matter concerning another member: She would pause as though to rummage through her mind. "I don't think I can say," would be her standard response. Dick chuckled at this. It usually satisfied the questioner, who believed she did not know. In actuality she merely was saying, that she was not at liberty to tell what she knew.

He had not told her all – or even many of – the details. He had simply explained that Irene had some strange events happening at her house, and he was trying to ease her concerns and see if there was some rational explanation for them. That had been enough.

As he stepped out the door, the cold blast of a Michigan winter hit him squarely in the face. He was tempted to start the car then return to the warmth of the parsonage until the engine had warmed up and the heater was putting forth some comfortable air. However, he really wanted this weekly trip to pass quickly so he could get on with the preparations of the holidays, so he turned the key and felt the jerk as the uncomfortably cold engine shook itself into action. Then he put the car in gear, backed out of the garage and headed for Irene's.

This old car must feel like a milk wagon horse, he laughed to himself. *The first stop on the weekend route. I wonder if I were to let go of the wheel, if it could find its own way.* The thought amused him, and he let himself drift back to early childhood days, when milk was delivered daily, the mailman actually walked his route, and the coal and ice man made regular deliveries. Ice in the summer. Coal in the winter.

He turned the corner of Irene's street, and pulled up to the curb. Major was nowhere to be seen. Actually Major had not bothered him since that first night's snarl. Still, Dick had tacitly felt that one of the bonus' of the post-Christmas absence of "Mother" would be the end of *Major watching* on his weekly arrival.

Irene answered the door almost as soon as Dick had knocked. She had come to expect his Saturday morning visits and – although she no longer interrupted his Friday evenings, she always was eager to see him and bring him up to date on "Mother."

"I called my sister to tell her about the light in my closet," she said, almost breathlessly. She asked me when the lights appeared. I told her Monday, Wednesday, Friday and every other Sunday. She said, 'Well that explains it. It's here on Tuesday, Thursday, Saturday and every other Sunday.'" She looked Dick squarely in the eye, and challenged him with, "What do you make of that, Pastor Dick?"

Dick, of course could make nothing of it. By now he felt trapped in the rabbit hole – well beneath the surface of reality. Still, he felt the need to assume some semblance of control. If he looked as bewildered as he felt, it would have been no help to Irene. It also would have made him appear to be as big a fool as he felt himself to be. *Appearances are everything,* he told himself as he fumbled for some response.

"The light simply stays in the closet and shines? It doesn't move about the house, or even wiggle?" he inquired as though the answer could possible be of use to him.

"No, it doesn't move from the closet. It only floats in place and shines rather dimly."

"Well, that is something. At least it poses no threat," Dick said as though he had made some significant observation. It was a rather lame attempt to maintain decorum while giving some assurance to Irene that there was no danger in its being there.

Quickly, he switched subjects, "There's only a week until Christmas, Irene. Your mother promised she would leave then. Perhaps she just wants to spend whatever time she has remaining with you and your sister." With this, Dick felt he had said something of value. There was no danger. It was just eerie – strange and unsettling. It would soon be over.

Dick sensed that Irene was quite upset by this latest turn of events. She asked him if he would care for some coffee, so he accepted and they chatted for about half an hour. Dick kept directing the conversation to family and holiday matters, and Irene kept trying to talk about spiritual realms and ghosts, and speculations on why someone would want to return to this realm if the spiritual was so desirable.

Dick actually wished to explore the same subject, but not with Irene. When this was all over he would seek out a professor he believed might be open to the subject.

Perhaps Dr. Walston would have some ideas on this. He was from England, and the British, he believed, had more experience with ghostly visitors.

They finished their coffee and their dialogical tug-of-war. Dick left with a feeling of hope. He could do nothing about whatever this was at Irene's. That was almost over, though. Then he could approach Dr. Walston. The man was a brilliant scholar – theologian. Surely he would be able to make some sense of this, so it would not haunt Dick over the years.

CHAPTER 20

It was Thursday morning. Two days until the Christmas Eve celebration. Dick had attended the rehearsal for the children's pageant the night before. The cardboard inn and cave had been dragged from their storage, dusted and repainted where necessary. The shepherds' robes were lengthened or shortened to fit this year's batch of fifth graders. Fortunately, Dick thought, the sanctuary was on the second floor and it was not practical to try to bring animals up the steep, winding steps. Thankfully, that decision finally had been made much earlier, after years of discussion between some of the local farmers and the board of trustees. Dick had learned this upon his arrival from a few farmers who still wished to revive the issue.

The angel chorus was composed of the usual fifth grade girls, many of whom actually did look like angels, although their voices were a bit unsure of some of the notes. All, in all it had promised to be another big night for this little village which so loved its children.

The phone rang, and Diane answered it with the usual cheery, "Methodist parsonage. Good morning!" (They had discussed adding "and God bless you," but decided that was not their style and it would come across as artificial). "Yes he is, *Irene*. I'll get him for you." She handed the phone to Dick with a look of dismay. She, too, would be glad when Christmas passed and "Mother" would go back to heaven – or hell – whichever."

"What's happening, Irene?" Dick skipped the pleasantries and cut to the chase. She called. There must be a reason.

"When I went in to Danny's bedroom this morning, the room was frigid. His heating vent had been closed. Danny did not close it. Neither did Walter."

"Perhaps Danny was too warm in the night and just decided to close it. He may have been too sleepy at the time to remember he did it." Irene was getting jumpy again. A closed heating vent is not the act of a disembodied spirit.

"Don't you remember, Pastor Dick. The house sits on a slab. There is no basement. The furnace is in the attic and the heating vents are in the ceiling. That's eight feet up. There is no way Danny could have reached it."

Dick hesitated. There was no point in driving over to stare at the ceiling vent. Danny could not have closed it. Walter did not close it, and Irene certainly did not want it closed. *What to say – what to do?* Finally he spoke in slow, controlled tones. "Irene, we have only three days more to go. This was a nuisance – not a danger. Just bear with it for a few more days. Then we will talk and put this episode to rest. Okay?"

"Well I don't know anything else to do. I know you can't do anything about it, but I wanted you to know." She paused then added. "I just had to tell someone."

This was it" Dick thought. *I've been reduced from probable protector to convenient confidant."* He hung up the phone and smiled lamely at Diane. "If Garrett ever offers a course in basic exorcism I'll take it."

She smiled and put her arm around him for comfort. They had entered this venture of ministry as a team. She had known then that her role was going to be a supporter. Neither she nor Dick had any clear idea of what this journey would mean or where it would lead them, physically, mentally or spiritually. It was something Dick felt he had to do, and she had spoken those words, "for better or for worse . . . till death do us part."

Dick appreciated her silent, steady support. He readily acknowledged that she was actually serving as resident pastor while he was the visiting preacher who blew in from Illinois every weekend. They stepped back and looked at each other with affection and suppressed laughter. "Whoever thought we'd be chasing ghosts when we took this on?" Dick asked rhetorically. Diane just nodded her head then turned her attention to preparing dinner while Dick headed for the study to polish up the Christmas Eve message.

Before looking at his sermon notes, Dick reflected upon the wonder of the Christmas tale. *The only thing Matthew and Luke agree on is the birth took place in Bethlehem,* he mused. *Everything else contradicts the other. Each picked up material from differing sources – every one of them wanting to believe that Jesus was that long-expected Messiah who would come from the birth place of King David. Perhaps,* he thought, *I should write my doctoral dissertation - if and when I get that far - on demonstrating that Jesus never was in Bethlehem.* He played with that thought for a moment then decided, *Nah, I don't want to be known as the Grinch who stole Christmas. Besides,* he reflected, *The Christmas story transcends history. It's the church's remembrance of Jesus. In him, they encountered both the human and the divine. 'O Little Town of Bethlehem .*

. . the hopes and fears of all the years were met in thee . . . that night.

The good people of his church wanted and deserved to hear Good News. God was and is involved in our lives. Life is not a tale told by an idiot, full of sound and fury and signifying nothing. It is a precious gift bestowed upon us by a benevolent deity – for reasons we can only speculate.

Strangely, Dick reflected, *this encounter with Irene's guest has put my ministry back in perspective. Perhaps Leonard was right: I have been spending too much time in my head and not enough in my soul. Whatever is in Irene's house – and I have to believe it is the spirit of her mother, had persuaded me that the spiritual realm is a reality. It precedes us and shall continue when this old earth has faded into oblivion. Jesus was one of those rarities who had one foot in that realm and one here on earth. How or why? . . . I simply do not know.*

I do know this, however. The people do not show up on a Sunday to hear theology. They come to encounter God – to be reassured of his love and to find some direction for their lives.

He rummaged through the messy pile of papers on his desk and found the sermon notes. Then he paused to resume a practice that once was a pre-sermon ritual, but – of late – had been neglected. He settled into meditative prayer. Slowly, the image of Christmases past began to emerge in his mind, and the words he would speak on Saturday began to form in his mind.

Chapter 21

The Sunday sermon had been on the text, "Behold I am doing a new thing!" It seemed the proper way to begin the New Year. For Dick, it held a special meaning. It was a new semester at Garrett with new classes, with new professors, and new challenges – and most importantly – it would be without "Mother" hanging around the house. *She's now just the ghost of Christmas Past,* Dick thought smugly.

Diane had given Dick some very encouraging feedback from the congregation. Some had told her that they had been either delighted or moved or inspired (depending upon the speaker) by Dick's last few sermons. The consensus was that they seemed to have a new power and new focus.

Dick accepted this gratefully, and decided he would reflect upon it later.

Bob had called on Sunday evening to tell Dick that he would have to return for a funeral on Wednesday. He would drive his car and pick up Ken and Ron, so he and Leonard could start later, and take highway 96. The weather was clear, so they could sail along at 70 mph and get to Evanston in less than four hours. Since it was registration day and Illinois was on Central Time, it meant that Leonard would not have to arrive until 9:00.

"Wheeeeeeeee! We get to sleep in!" Dick said when he put down the phone.

To celebrate this minor victory, Diane defrosted a pizza, Deb pulled out a game board, and they played, laughed, and teased one another until late into the night.

Just as Diane saw Leonard's car pull up to the door, the phone rang. Diane picked it up to avoid Dick being caught in a prolonged phone conversation that might throw them off schedule. "Methodist parsonage. Good Morning!" she said cheerily. Then she paused. "Well, yes he is. Irene. He's about to leave for seminary though. Is it important?" With a look of resignation, she handed the phone to Dick.

"Good morning, Irene. What's happening?"

"Last night I woke up at about 3 A.M. with a strange feeling. I went into the kitchen and saw that all of the stove top burners were blazing bright red." Irene paused; then announced: "She's still here!"

CHAPTER 22

Immediately after registering for classes, Dick stopped by Dr. Walston's office to make an appointment. As luck would have it, Dr. Walston was in his office and he had some free time.

"Come in, Dick! Did you sign up for any of my courses this time around?" Dr. Walston was brilliant, but his specialty was systematic theology and Dick was not interested so much in learning a system as in seeing how systems developed and evolved. Historical theology allowed one to delve into the whys. He wanted to take a course from him, but it would have to be a reading course, one designed for discussion and exploration.

"Not this time, Dr. Walston." My reason for wanting to talk with you may seem rather odd, but I am hoping you can help me." Dr. Walston signaled for Dick to take a seat and as he did so, Dick breathed a sigh of relief, pulled out his notes and began relating the entire episode to Dr. Walston, beginning with the phone inquiry about a poltergeist.

Dr. Walston sat, listening to Dick, puffing nothing from his signature Sherlock Holmes-styled pipe that was his trade mark among the students. Whenever he was asked a tricky or involved question, Dr. Walston always pulled out his pipe, gave a few imaginary puffs while he organized his thoughts. Apparently he thought that was far more dignified than merely staring into space and muttering to himself. Dick watched him puffing and it assured him that he was being taken seriously.

When Dick finished his detailed narration, Dr. Walston took a few more puffs, set the pipe back in his jacket pocket, leaned forward and in an almost conspiratorial whisper said, "Dick, I wish I had been in your place for this. What you've told me certainly is extraordinary . . . but I believe every word of it."

Dick felt another wave of relief surge through his body. Just the act of finally being able to tell someone this fantastic story had lifted a burden from him. Now, to have the affirmation – from a respected professor – that he was not losing his mind – or suffering some terrible delusions – felt better than an unexpected A+ on a term paper.

"Thank you, Dr. Walston – for listening – and believing." Dick said with genuine emotion. "My question now is, where do I go for help from here? Mother is still hanging around the house and she is misbehaving."

Dr. Walston unconsciously pulled his pipe from its resting place and gave a few absent-minded puffs while considering the question. I don't know any exorcists personally, but I do have a few contacts that might be able to give some direction. I'll check on it today, Dick, and try to get back to you before Friday. Will that be satisfactory?"

Dick almost hugged him for that, but settled for, "Should I contact you or will you get in touch with me?"

"I'll contact you, Dick – with this condition: I sit in with you when you meet whomever I am able to enlist."

"Done!"

"I'll be in touch."

Dick went directly to the book store to purchase the required reading for his courses. This term he would begin some of his doctoral courses while completing those required for his masters. Eusebius' *Church History* I and II, in classical Greek. "What a way to start!" Church Administration, Urban Sociology, and the Pauline Letters. He was also taking a reading course for his preaching credits, but those books would be selected in consultation with the professor. Most required only one text, fortunately. Church Administration required a copy of the Discipline. *It's time I read it to find out what I should have been doing these past few years,* he thought as he signed to charge.

Once back in his room he began to sort the reading on the two desks the room contained. *History and preaching on the right. The rest on the left*, he decided. The room was too cramped to accommodate two students, but it did have two desks. This allowed Dick the luxury of dividing his studies and taking a mental break from some when turning to the others. Since the desks were at opposite ends of the room, some evenings he felt he got his exercise merely by striding from one desk to the other.   Before the second week both desks would be cluttered with opened, upside down books sprawling across whatever open space remained from the class notes and private scribblings.

Neatness was never my forte, he decided as he surveyed the already disorderly array, turned and left the room, headed for the library. Now that he technically was a doctoral student he had to reserve a carrel in the stacks as a place to begin his research.

Finally, with all the registration day chores completed, Dick went to the main lobby, sat down and waited for the carpool bunch to arrive for the dinner cruise. They had agreed much earlier that the first night of each term would be spent cruising for a new dining spot. This was one of their techniques for breaking up the tedium of a stale menu. They had searched out Italian, Mexican, Greek, and Korean. They had found a great place for fish, another for pancakes, one for ribs, and another for down-home cookin' complete with greens and grits.

Dick was far more concerned with what Dr. Walston would come up with, however, than in any of the culinary accomplishments they might encounter. Some inner sense of excitement had been growing in him since he heard from Irene about mother's last visit. Something terribly sinister was at work there, he felt. He also had this vague sense of everything gathering for a dramatic climax. He had moved from skeptic to believer; from protector to confidant; and from someone who was self-confident in his ability to solve any problem with his mind – to a mental stumble-bum with no idea of what was going on – or what to do about it. *Shakespeare's Hamlet was right, 'There are more things in heaven and earth than are dreamt of in your philosophy, Horatio" . . . or" Dick." The mind can only carry us so far. We live in a mystery that is totally incomprehensible. How any person or council could ever muster the colossal arrogance to decide that they and they alone understood the true nature of God and Christ is beyond me.*

Ken showed up first. Then Bob and finally, Leonard. Ron had opted out some time back, preferring the inexpensive and reliable fare at the dining hall.

Bob kicked off the quest: "Let us venture forth in search of food that will tantalize the palate and nurture our frail bodies."

"Frail, doesn't quite describe it," offered Ken. "My car groans with relief every time this group unloads."

They searched the back streets of Evanston and eventually located an inexpensive steak house with a remarkably tender and delicious selection.

Once settled into the dinner, they picked up their God Maker seminar.

"Okay, great teacher," Ken smiled as he said it, "What lesson do we have tonight?"

"Just one word: 'Salvation.' I think it needs to be dropped from our vocabulary."

"Hey, isn't that what we're about: Bringing salvation – or at least offering salvation to the people?" Leonard asked this almost tentatively, knowing Dick was laying some sort of intellectual trap, and realizing as he spoke that he probably had stepped into it.

"Let go back to Jesus' parable we call the Prodigal Son, which defined the forgiving nature of God. If we believe it, then what is the need for salvation? Paul said it clearly in Romans 8:31: 'If God is on our side, who is against us?' and again in 8:33 'If God pronounces acquittal; then who can condemn?'"

Leonard added, "And he ends the passage with those beautiful words: 'For I am convinced that there is nothing in death or in life, in the realm of spirits or superhuman powers, in the world as it is or the world as it shall be, in the forces of the universe'" . . . as if on cue, the rest joined Leonard in reciting, "'in heights or depths – nothing in all creation that can separate us from the love of God in Christ Jesus our Lord.."'

They sat quietly, letting the full impact of the meaning of those words sink into their consciousness.

"Then what is this 'Salvation' bit?" Dick asked almost in a whisper.

"Life is a journey. I am totally convinced that this earthly portion is but a brief part of that journey – or pilgrimage really. I simply cannot believe that these few years are going to be the determining factor in how we spend eternity. My God does not operate that way. For one thing I realize I am nowhere near capable of living in eternal bliss. I still have too much self-centeredness, competitiveness, envy, lust, greed – Get the idea? There is no way I - or anyone I know could be satisfied in Paradise or any other place as we are. I've known very wealthy people who could have everything their hearts desired, who are miserable creatures. What in Paradise is going to change that? When people tell me they've been saved, what they tell me is that they think their journey is over – done with – finished. They've arrived! Thinking you've been saved stops a person well short of the finish line. Add to all this Paul's statement in 2 Corinthians 1, 'God was in Christ reconciling the world to himself, not counting their trespasses (remember trespass is a stronger word than sin. It's intentional) against them, but calling us to be agents of reconciliation.' Reconciling suggests an ongoing process, with completion or wholeness as the goal not just escape from punishment."

"But, Dick," Ken interrupted, "Wesley spoke of perfecting grace following saving grace. Once we understand and accept God's forgiveness, we move on to perfection – which really means completion or wholeness."

"Good point, Ken, but why go through the unnecessary and damaging process of believing ourselves to be guilty in God's eyes and needing God's forgiveness, rather than accepting God's unconditional, loving acceptance and moving forward, learning from our failures? Jesus does not save us from God's wrath. He teaches us how to save ourselves from our own failures or sins. God does not consign his children to Hell. We create our own hell through our egocentricity. Besides," Dick added, "few preachers proclaim 'perfecting grace' these days, and even fewer Christians understand or strive for it."

Finally, Bob spoke up: "Okay, Dick, supposing you're right. What are we supposed to be doing as spiritual leaders?"

"Asked and answered, as a lawyer would say, Bob. 'Spiritual leaders.' is the key term. I really do not believe most of us lead people spiritually. We can't guide people to where we ourselves haven't gone. We confuse religion with spirituality. Religion gives people a framework for understanding their world and for knowing what is expected of them. Spirituality is living, at least in part, within the spiritual realm. It is being in touch with The Divine. I've lost a lot of that while becoming better versed in our 'religion.'"

With this, he paused to let the implications of his confession soak in – to others and himself. This encounter with Irene's 'poltergeist' had opened some doors he had closed along the way, and he was trying to find his way back.

"The endless journey," Bob muttered quietly as he picked up his knife and began to carve slices of the steak before him.

Leonard smiled silently and stuffed a piece of medium rare into his mouth.

Chapter 23

Dr. Walston paged Dick on the school intercom on Tuesday morning. He had contacted a Catholic priest, Father Milton, who came highly recommended as an authority on disembodied spirits. Assuming the urgency of the situation, Dr. Walston had taken the liberty of setting up a luncheon on Wednesday, at noon. 11:00 was chapel time and Dick could afford to skip the 1:00 which was Church Administration. It would only be an orientation session, passing out assignments and scheduling reports.

The restaurant selected by Dr. Walston was one of the finer dining places in Evanston. Dick realized the tab would be his, and he hoped his guests would have modest appetites. Father Milton looked like someone directly out of a Hollywood casting company. He appeared to be in his early 70's, slightly stooped in posture, with a beautiful, almost cascading shock of silver-grey hair, flowing down to his shoulders. His nose resembled a rooster beak, and his eyes were a faded bluish hue. He wore a slightly frayed clerical collar, atop his stark, black suit.

They quickly dispensed with the niceties, placed their orders, and settled into the matter at hand.

"I purposefully did not ask Dr. Walston for many details, Dick, because I wanted to hear your account with fresh ears."

"How much do you want to know?"

"How much do you feel would be helpful for me to understand the situation?"

Touche, thought Dick. *This man is experienced. I might as well start from the beginning and give every little detail.*

Father Milton listened intently as Dick relayed every detail. He had brought along his notes to be sure of the sequence. The narration continued through the salad and soup courses. Dick took his time, because the soup was delicious, and he did not want it becoming tepid while he chatted. So he would stop from time to time as for effect, while lapping up the wonderful concoction of mushroom and brie in cream sauce.

When Dick got to the part about the ouija board, Father Milton, sighed, "Oh dear. Has it begun to swear yet?"

Dick almost spit his mouthful of soup across the table, but managed to mildly choke on it instead. "Well, yes, it has," he acknowledged.

Father Milton turned to Dr. Walston and confided, "They always do that. Somewhere along the way they begin to swear." Then he turned to Dick. Looked him straight in the eye and instructed: "You will have to be very firm with the board. Tell it that if it swears again you will throw the board away and never speak to it again."

"I did that," Dick acknowledged," mentally slapping himself on the forehead in disbelief. He had done the proper thing, in spite of himself - - -albeit for the wrong reason.

"Did the board identify who was speaking and why they were there?" Father Milton inquired.

"Yes," Dick replied, "It claimed to be Irene's mother and said she was there out of love."

"Oh another one of those," Father Milton said in dismay. Then he leaned back and both Dick and Dr. Walston knew they were in for an interesting lecture on departed spirits.

"There are no pearly gates or angels strumming harps from personal clouds. It's an entirely different realm of being than what we experience here. Let's let it go at that for now. Some people never adjusted well to being here. They always were wanting to be somewhere else. You might call them 'restless souls.' Well, they could not adjust to this life and now they can't adjust to the other life any better, so they are always trying to find a way to return to this one. You see them everywhere in this earthly, physical existence. They talk about how good it was where they used to be . . . even though they never thought so when they were there."

He paused to let this sink in, then pointed to four ladies who were at an adjoining table. All four were talking at the same time.

"Do you see those ladies? If this place were to blow up into little pieces, they would sit there talking forever if someone did not come and direct them to where they need to go."

Dick looked at Dr. Walston, who smiled and nodded a tacit agreement.

"Everyone does not take easily to living in the spirit realm. There are a variety of reasons for disembodied spirits continuing to dwell here in the physical realm. Some are traumatized and cannot get past the moment of their death and the events that caused it. They are the miserable ones, moaning and groaning and frightening people out of their wits. They're searching for something they can never find and refuse all attempts to help them to adjust to their new mode of being. Others have trouble letting go of their things or their relationships."

He paused long enough to take a sip of his coffee. Dick hoped he would begin to work on his fillet. The thought of that much money going directly to the garbage can was distracting him from the point of the meeting. He idly wondered if they could ask for a doggie bag. Then he regained his focus, and as if on cue, Father Milton continued.

Suddenly, Father Milton changed pace: "Has liquid begun disappearing from sealed bottles yet?" he inquired with some urgency.

"Not to my knowledge. Why?"

"It will – probably soon now. It's the spirit's way of letting people know of its presence. It also shows that their power is increasing. It requires strong power to make a liquid disappear. Making lights and moving ouija board markers is rather elementary."

"Then there are those who feel they have unfinished business. Stop and think about it, " he interjected, "We all have unfinished business. No one has ever said everything he wanted to say to everyone he knew, and every one of us has some uncompleted projects laying around. Still, these lost souls have control issues, some compulsiveness which causes them to believe the world cannot get by if they do not do everything they believed they were to do. So," he said with a sad sigh, "we have these spirits hovering where they do not belong, also."

"Mother giving her reason as love is just so much hogwash. My bet is she is a control freak. If she had been alive when Danny was born she would have been one of those, 'Mother knows best how to raise children,' grandmothers. You said she was talking with Danny long before Irene knew of her presence. Children seem to have a quality of seeing spirits far better than adults can. There are various theories as to why this is so. Just take my word for it, if a child thinks he is talking to a ghost, he probably is."

"If what you say is true," interjected Dr. Walston, "then why don't we have far more of these disembodied spirits than we do?"

"Oh, we have far more than people realize. Most just tend to behave themselves and not bother those who happen to live near them."

"So how do we get rid of 'Mother,' Father Milton? Do you do exorcisms, or is there something we can do?" Dick thought he had learned far more than he needed to about spirits. The point of the meeting was to try to get rid of Irene's. This had been interesting, to be sure. *If I leave without making some arrangement to help Irene, then this had really just been an entertaining waste of time . . . and money,* he thought woefully.

"I don't do the exorcism myself," Father Milton explained. "I have a colleague, a former nun, who does the actual exorcism." Dick silently wondered why they had spent their time with the priest instead of the nun, but said nothing. He waited for the other shoe to fall. This was it: The pitch. Father Milton was her agent. Sister what-ever-her-name-was would do the exorcism for x number of dollars. He could hear it now. Then he would have to tell Irene the cost. If she agreed, then he would pray fervently that it worked or he would have been part of an elaborate con.

Before he had time to fret further, Father Milton added, " She will do this for mere travel, food ,and housing. I accompany her to assist if needed, and I make no charge either. We have dedicated our lives to helping people like Irene whose lives have been disrupted by these poor lost souls. In the process we also help the soul to find its way home, as well.

Dick felt a twinge of embarrassment. And wondered if Father Milton had anticipated his concern or if he had been capable of . . . *No way!* Dick thought. *Let's not make this whole thing eerier than it already is.*

"I'm sure that Irene has room to put you both up, and I can furnish the transportation. I'll check with Irene and we will set up a time. In fact, let's plan on next weekend if that fits with your schedule."

"Agreed," said Father Milton, and he leaned back and took another sip of his now tepid coffee.

How does the exorcism actually work?" Dick asked. As he did so, Dick noticed Dr. Walston pull his pipe from his jacket pocket and begin puffing imaginary smoke rings.

"It's really extremely simple, Dick. We don't use bells and incense – or incantations. Sister Martha simply calls up the spirit. Once she is certain it is present, she says.:

> 'You are dead.!
> You do not belong here.
> Go back to where you came from!'""

"That's it?" Dr. Walston asked.

Father Milton nodded. "That's it. It has to be said firmly and with authority. Then the spirit merely turns and goes back to where it came from."

"Sounds simple." Dick observed.

"Life is simple," said Father Milton. "We humans just make it more complicated than it should be."

Dr. Walston nodded agreement and returned his pipe to his jacket pocket.

The waiter came with the bill. Dick took it, and then decided to also take a sip of coffee before seeing what this experience had cost him. *Oh, the cost of discipleship!* he thought, as he lifted the bill and glanced at the bottom line.

Chapter 24

No need to visit Irene this morning, Dick thought. *I'll just give her a call and tell her I can have her certified exorcists here by next Friday evening. She'll find some way to house them, even if she has to ship Danny off to the neighbors.* Dick was certain of that.

He had told the carpool that he would need to bring some extra passengers home. It was Bob's turn to drive, so it would work perfectly. Leonard would drive with Dick and the rest could go in Bob's car. At seminary, they would use Bob's car for dinner excursions. It would only cost Dick the price of gasoline. After the restaurant bill, that looked like a very minor expense, at worst.

Irene answered the phone. *Walter never answers the phone,* Dick realized. *I'm not sure I ever heard him speak, yet I know he's argued with Irene, so he's not a mute.*

"Irene, I have the priest and nun who will expel Mother from the house," said Dick, with a feeling of satisfaction, bordering on pride. He had intentionally identified the couple as a priest and nun, assuming this would give some extra credibility to his claim.

"Oh, thank God – and thank you, Pastor Dick," Irene said with obvious gratitude and relief. "The strangest thing happened this week." She paused, and Dick held his breath. *Let's not let anything mess up this weekend,* he thought. "What was that?" he asked innocently.

"I gave Walter a bottle of after shave lotion for Christmas," she began. Dick could hear it coming even before she got the words out of her mouth. "Last night I saw the bottle and it is half empty." She waited a moment as if to compose herself. "The bottle is unopened, Pastor Dick. The plastic wrap is still in place around the cap."

"They do that as their power increases, Irene. It's just their way of letting you know of their presence. There's really nothing to worry about." As soon as the words left his mouth, Dick had that too familiar feeling. Everything made sense and nothing made sense. He really was living on the other side of the looking glass.

"Are you sure?" was her only rejoinder.

"Father Milton told me we could expect this to happen." Dick replied, again wanting to slap his own head in disbelief. *The Mad Hatter must be around here somewhere. But if he is, I don't want to know about it. Mother is enough of a problem right now.*

They continued to talk and Irene agreed to house Father Milton and his nun colleague.

Dick did not bother to go into the details of how the exorcism would work. He actually hoped Sister Martha would jazz it up a bit for Irene's benefit.

CHAPTER 25

Leonard came by at 7:15 A.M. Since they were not picking up the rest of the carpool they could take highway 96 and save more than enough time to make it to class before the bell rang.

Dick realized he had some explaining to do to Leonard. When he loaded the priest and nun into the car on Friday morning, some explanation would have to be given. This was a time for some trust. He did not want to start a series of lies. Truth – but not the whole truth - seemed the order of the day.

"Leonard, I need to level with you about what has been going on in Napoleon these past few months."

"About time, I'd say, Dick. It's been obvious to me that something has been troubling you. I figured if you wanted me to know you would tell me. Still, I thought you needed to tell someone, and I assumed you and I had a pretty good friendship going for us."

Leonard had been more of a friend than he realized in many ways. Dick was heavily into academics. He hung out with the intellectuals and debated and discussed esoteric theories and obscure manuscripts as though the whole of Christendom depended upon his getting and proclaiming the correct understanding. Leonard, on the other hand, had a simple faith. Love, trust and helpfulness was his trinity. The professors were not impressed by him, but his congregation loved him – confided in him –

relied upon him. This awareness kept drawing Dick back from abstract theology to practical ministry.

"I made a promise not to reveal the family or the details because of the ruckus it might cause. I can tell you this much, though: The people I am bringing back with us are coming to do an exorcism. Now don't tell anyone – including your family about this, okay?"

Leonard just shook his head as though to clear away whatever had invaded his mind. "Okay, Dick. I assume you know what you're doing. That's good enough for me."

Again, Leonard had demonstrated why Dick had taken an instant liking to this diamond-in-the-rough farmer-turned-preacher.

"Do you want to wrestle some more with your God Makers' theory?"

"Sure. Let's do."

"Let's start with this idea: There is a significant difference between a religion and a spiritual journey. Jesus did not come to start a new religion or establish a new church. He came to proclaim the Kingdom (or nation) of God in our midst. He said, 'Repent,' which simply meant 'transform the way you think,' and you will find yourself living in that kingdom - in the fellowship of God your Father."

"I believe he came to put us on the right path of our personal spiritual journey. But because of the early interpreters I mentioned, we found ourselves bogged down in a system of sin and salvation. Most of what takes place in the churches I know has little to do with one's spiritual journey into a relationship with God as Father."

"Hey, wait a minute, Dick. I know a lot of very decent people in our churches."

"Decent has nothing to do with one's spiritual journey, Leonard. Check the Scriptures. Jesus never told people to be good. He called them to wholeness. He called them to shed their egocentricity and learn to care for, and about, others. He called people into community. What we have today is a patchwork of morality posing as Christianity. We once thought Christians did not dance or drink or play cards – or work on Sunday. We allowed slavery and wars of aggression like the Crusades. We have denominations claiming to be the only true church because of some heritage or particular way of handling a liturgy. God doesn't give a hoot about those things. Window trimming. That's all it is."

"'Love mercy. Do justly. Walk humbly with your God.' Maybe that does sum it up, Dick." Leonard said.

"It's that walk humbly with God bit that's the trick. I believe God is as much a part of our being as our breath. We are never alone, and we are never without guidance if we open ourselves to it. We also have access to a greater power than we realize if we are willing to work to discover it. All that is a part of spirituality. Being good is what follows naturally. That should not be our focus in worship – or the thrust of our sermons. Most sermons I hear in the preaching classes are filled with 'shoulds and oughts.' "

Leonard seemed to ponder this for a moment, then he added: "The word of God for the people of God. Thus says the Lord," He said this quietly – almost reverently in a somewhat bewildered response.

"Too much of what comes from the pulpits does not jibe with our personal experience and beliefs. We give the answers the professors – or our *favorite* professors gave to us – whether we believe them or not, and we call it preaching. I know a couple of guys who took two sermons into their preaching exams. They waited to see which professors were grading them before selecting the sermon. Can you imagine the integrity they must show when the chairman of their pastor/parish committee who sets their salaries – or the chair of the parsonage committee is sitting in the pew?"

Dick let this sink in as they drove in silence for a few miles.

"Leonard, I fear for our church. I really do. Far too many think the ministry is a safe job. For too many pew sitters, church is an acquired habit or a place to gather with friends. I take heart when I see men like you and Bob and Ken, and some of the other guys at Garrett. However, I see too many who found a place to hide during the Viet Nam War – too many who drifted into the ministry as a steady, secure haven. I watch with horror as I see a new breed appearing on television. These guys are nothing but snake oil salesmen, appealing to people's piety. For them, it pays - big time - to love Jesus. When I look back at our history I see a church which has been both a saint and a whore."

He drove on, smoldering silently.

"God is too great. Jesus Christ – too wonderful a person. Life too precious. Death too certain. There is a substance of hope and power that can change lives if we do it correctly, Leonard.."

"Jesus tried and they crucified him, Dick." Leonard spoke simply. "All we can do is tend the little plot given to us. Prepare the soil as well as we can. Make sure that what we plant is authentic, and pray for the best."

"Pick the best seeds. Plow the furrows straight. Tend the farm. Let your neighbors do as they will. Leonard., my friend, you should be a philosopher . . . No., let me correct that: You *are* a philosopher."

Leonard smiled and picked up one of his text books, cracked it open and began trying to get ahead in his reading.

They drove the rest of the way in quiet contemplation: Leonard of his reading assignment and Dick in balancing his idealism with Leonard's practicality. He had the distinct impression that Leonard had made a point: Sometimes, perhaps, wisdom beats intelligence.

CHAPTER 26

The week passed without incident. It was the usual early-in-the-term schedule. Dick began selecting the themes for the major papers, and setting completion dates for each. He knew it was far too early to even consider a dissertation subject. Still, his major interest was in Patristic studies and how the doctrines of Christology and Trinity had developed during those first four centuries of the Church. He spent some time browsing through the old stacks just to see what was available. He was amazed at the selection. There were books dating from the 1800's written by scholars who appeared to have excellent command of the Greek, as well as a detailed understanding of the events of the patristic period of the Church. His appetite was whetted and he could hardly wait for the time when he would be free to do his own original research.

On Wednesday, they had returned to the recently discovered steak house, and decided it would be a weekly feature.

On Thursday evening, someone reported that the weather prediction was for heavy snow. Everyone groaned at the news. This would mean slower driving conditions, so Friday evening dinners would be delayed. Dick checked with Father Milton, and set the time and place to pick up him and Sister Martha for the long – now very long – ride to Napoleon. He was glad he had leveled with Leonard about the purpose of his extra riders. This would give them all something to talk about on the trip, and relieve some of the tedium.

When Dick awoke on Friday morning, he immediately was aware of a profound silence. Not a sound – anywhere! He looked out his dorm window and what he saw caused his heart to sink: Snow was everywhere. Not just some flakes scattered about, but snow – piled up, covering the lower windows, blocking the doors. He turned on his radio and heard the announcer say: "Twenty three inches of the cold white stuff fell on Chicago last night, my friends. Just stay home, and stay warm. Nobody is going anywhere today. Chicago is snow-bound." *Good grief!*, thought Dick. *I better call Diane and have her call our lay leader, Walt, and tell him he has a sermon to preach Sunday.*

Fortunately for Dick, snow had blown away from his dorm. The doors on the other side of the yard were barely visible because the snow had piled up to about five feet. Custodians and students joined in to free the students trapped in there. At first there was some discussion as to whether it would be better to dig or to tunnel. Digging was settled on and a strange bucket-brigade line formed. The ones closest to the doors threw their load of snow back toward the yard, and then those farther back threw that load even farther, so it would not pile up and create a barrier.

Eventually everyone was freed and they all headed to the main dorm where breakfast was being served over an indefinitely extended period.

Dick returned to his dorm to call Father Milton and tell him the obvious. "I'll have to reschedule for next week," he said.

"We can't do it next weekend, Dick. We already made plans to help a family in Iowa. We'll just have to get out our joint calendars and set another time, after you have had the opportunity to talk with Irene."

The weekend and next week passed far too slowly for all who had missed their expected family weekend. Dick had called home and spoken with each of the girls, telling them that they would do something special when he came home the next weekend. He had no idea what that "something special" would be, but at least he had a week to come up with something.

It took the entire week before the streets were clear and the cars were able to be driven. Snow was piled high everywhere. Two-lane streets were one-lane and drivers were forced to practice unaccustomed courtesy.

On Thursday evening a weather report said there was a possibility of another "big snow" hitting the area during the night. A quick conference of the carpool arrived at a unanimous decision. They bundled themselves into the two cars after their last class and headed out of the city. Whatever was being taught the next day could remain a mystery.

They were headed home!

CHAPTER 27

It was nearly 9:00 when Dick pulled up to the parsonage said goodbye to Leonard and opened the door. He had called ahead, so they were expecting him and would not be concerned about a car pulling up or a door opening at a late hour.

This time all three of his "girls " were lined up and ready for hugs. Deb, then Cindy, then Diane. Each one received his full attention and affection in turn.

The girls had eaten earlier, but Diane had waited for Dick to arrive. They all sat at the table, everyone chattering at once, vying for attention and wanting to share their stories. Dick had a quick deja-vu moment, recalling the four women he had seen chattering at the restaurant, and he could appreciate what they, perhaps, had been experiencing.

The girls had to get to bed almost immediately as they still had school. Dick promised them a trip to the movies for a late afternoon matinee and then a trip to the pizza parlor. They squealed with delight at this, and went upstairs to dress for bed. Dick and Diane gave them about five minutes then followed their path for evening prayers, songs and kisses.

Afterwards, they sat and cuddled in front of the television, paying little, if any, attention to whatever was playing. The time apart had been too long . They needed to spend these moments rediscovering one another before they, too, retired to their bed.

After the girls had left for school. Dick decided it was safe to call Irene. He really did not want people to know he was home yet. His sermon was prepared (it was the one he had prepared for the previous week). But he wanted just to be free of any responsibility – either at the church or at school – for one, peaceful day. Irene would not be one to tell anybody of his call. She wanted their conversations to remain as private as possible.

"Good morning, Irene. I drove home last night to avoid another possible blizzard. We need to schedule another time for Father Milton and Sister Martha to come."

"Pastor Dick," Irene almost interrupted him. "Something very, very strange happened last Friday."

Dick waited, wondering what else could happen, as Irene seemed to be gathering her thoughts.

"I heard Mother's voice!"

"How did that happen?"

"She was talking with Danny. He could see her, but I could only hear her. It *was* her voice. *It really was my mother*!"

Dick felt his flesh crawling as a sudden chill flashed through his body.

"I called to her and demanded, 'Mother, what are you still doing here? You promised you would leave after Christmas.'"

Dick had an impulse to ask what her reply was, but realized he was about to receive the answer without his prompting.

"She said, 'I'm not going back until I can take Danny with me.' Suddenly everything made sense: The closed heating vent; the stove top burners blazing red hot heat! She was trying to kill Danny so he could be with her."

Dick waited, almost holding his breath, waiting to hear what followed.

"I said to her – actually I yelled at her – 'Mother you are dead. You do not belong here. Go back to where you belong!'"

Upon hearing those words, Dick almost called out from some inner excitement. He waited, however, for Irene to continue her tale.

"Then I felt a strange quietness. Oh, the house wasn't noisy before. This was more like a quietness of presence. Mother was gone! *I knew it*! There was an emptiness and feeling of peace in its place." She paused then continued: "Everything has been quiet since that moment, Pastor Dick. She is gone! At last, she is gone!" Irene spoke this with such a sense of relief Dick could see the tears in her eyes as she said the words.

"Wheeew!" Dick breathed a sigh of relief, himself. "Get rid of that ouija board, Irene. Throw it out and never – do you hear me? – *never* use one again. I am going to call Father Milton, if he is still in Chicago. Then I will come over. We need to talk."

Dick hung up and gave Diane a you'll-never-belief-this stare. Then he dialed Father Milton's number. He assumed Diane would hear his conversation and learn what just happened without the need to tell the story twice.

"Father Milton, here. Can I help you?"

"Father Milton, this is Dick. I just spoke with Irene and you will never believe – I mean you will never believe – what she just told me." Without waiting for a reply, Dick told the entire story, emphasizing the exorcism formula recited by Irene, although Dick knew and assured Father Milton that he had never told Irene those details.

He waited, and though no words were spoken he could hear Father Milton saying to himself, "I'll be damned!". Finally Father Milton broke his silence. "Tell her to get rid of the ouija board," he ordered.

"I already did that." One more time, Dick mentally slapped his forehead – not believing that he was still correctly playing his part in this Alice-in-Wonderland drama.

He set down the phone and stared at Diane one more time. "It's over, then? "she asked.

"Seems so. I'm going over to talk with Irene now. Then this afternoon we'll take in a movie and try to wash this strange episode out of our minds."

"I don't think it's going to be that easy to forget this," Diane offered.

"Probably not," agreed Dick as he headed out the door for one final trip to Irene's.

He took a look around for Major, and walked quickly to the door. Irene seemed to have been watching for him, for she opened the door even before he had set foot on the porch.

"Come in, Pastor Dick. I've made fresh coffee."

Dick was glad he had not had a second cup. He was learning that coffee nerves were an occupational illness for visiting pastors.

Irene thanked Dick for his attempts, then asked him directly, "Pastor Dick, what do you think was happening here?"

Dick breathed a long sigh, and looked at Irene: "I really don't know. Whatever it was lies beyond any experience I have ever had. I tried every logical explanation, as you well know." He shrugged as if in defeat. "But every last one of them fell apart."

Irene smiled with just a trace of satisfaction. "I know you were the skeptic, Pastor Dick. I began to count on that, and upon you finding some rational explanation for what was happening. Frankly, I was both a bit disappointed and a bit pleased when you failed. I suppose there is some truth in misery loving company. The fact that you also were baffled made me feel better about myself – though very uncomfortable."

Dick smiled back at Irene. This was a time for honesty. They were two weary veterans of the same struggle sharing their true feelings, now that the battle was over and done with.

"It was a tough lesson, but I relearned something I'd forgotten. There is a spiritual dimension out there – somewhere. It's every bit as real as the physical world in which we now live. That is our true home. As much as I find it distasteful to admit it, your mother was here. How she got here I have no idea. Still, she was here, and she was a force to be reasoned with."

Irene nodded. "She certainly proved to be. I don't know how she expected a closed vent and hot burners to kill Danny. There was nothing the burners could set fire to."

"Perhaps she was just testing – making preparations. If she could make liquid disappear from a sealed bottle, perhaps she thought she would soon be able to move some papers onto the stove."

This possibility startled Dick as he spoke it. He had no idea where his thought was going when he started it. Irene, also, looked shocked at the thought.

"Well, she's gone now. She can't do us any harm from where she's at."

"Remember the formula if she reappears." He hastened to add: "Don't say it now – or ever again, unless you need to," he cautioned.

"Good thought, Pastor Dick. Better to leave everything behind." She arose and offered Dick her hand. "Thank you for staying with me during this ordeal. Walter, as you know, was not much help. I needed someone to turn to – even if you were as confused as I was."

They smiled at one another. Dick took her hand. "Let's hope the next time you call it's just church business."

A bond had formed. It was a bond of friendship – much as might be formed by survivors of a shipwreck or a major accident.

"I'll see myself out, Irene. You get on with your day. See you in church," he added as he opened the door and stepped out into the cold morning.

He took one last look for Major (he assumed he would not make this trip again) and went to his car. He turned the ignition switch, heard the starter struggle against the cold, then the engine caught hold. He decided to let the car warm up a bit before putting it in gear. In actuality he wanted a moment to himself to reflect on what he had learned from this once-in-a-lifetime-episode. He understood that this experience would continue to unfold and teach him new lessons through the coming years. Still, there were some things he realized he had learned already, and they needed to be articulated and put in place.

We really are spiritual beings – presently undergoing a physical experience. This no longer is a matter of faith. That was Irene's mother. *Like it or not, I know her spirit – or soul – was residing in that house. I have no idea what the spirit world looks like – or where it exists. This I do know: A spiritual realm exists as surely as this physical one exists. Life beyond this one no longer is a matter of faith for me. It is simply a fact I accept.*

Love is such a precious gift. It may come in very different forms, but whatever shape it takes it should be treasured. Deb rushes to greet me, but is willing to step aside to allow me to give and receive love with others. Cindy sits fearfully waiting for my reassuring touch, but is able to offer comfort when she senses my need. Diane is whatever I require at the moment. I could not begin to accomplish what I do without her, and she sets her desires aside for me. Good friends like Leonard and others genuinely care about what happens to me. They listen to me, call me to account, and are willing to extend themselves to help me along life's path. In his mind he measured this with Walter's indifference and Irene's mother whose selfishness would slay Danny to kidnap him from his parents. *I can never take my family's love – or anyone's love - for granted again.*

You only learn the rudiments from a book or in a classroom, Dick. Life is the real classroom, and you have to stay open – and curious - to what it offers. There is a mystery and marvel about every facet of creation. That, too, should never be taken for granted. A closed mind misses the meaning of living. Intellectual arrogance is just another form of closed mindedness. Admitting your ignorance is the beginning of learning.

When you proclaim the gospel, make it relevant to life. People do not want abstract theology. They want hope – they want to experience the love and presence of God in their life. Don't ever – ever - act like the answer man. None of us has answers that easily transfer to someone else's questions. Your task is to help the people find their way through their problems and create their own workable relationship with God. As Paul put it to the Philippians: "You must work out your own salvation in fear and trembling."

God Maker, you are not! . . . *at least you should not be.* Dick felt an inner twinge of satisfaction as he acknowledged this. *You can share your image or vision, but don't ever pretend it is more than that. There are those whose images and understandings come from other cultures – other religions. If they have been faithfully thought out and tested by experience, you have no right – no basis except your own prejudice and narrowness of experience – for dismissing them. Rather, you might learn from them and be able to enlarge your own image and understanding of this ultimate mystery we call God.*

With that, he smiled wearily to himself, put the car in gear and began his drive homeward. He took a deep breath, as he pulled away from Irene's house. He was going back to the right side of the looking glass. He was going home. This time, he hoped he would have a better understanding of how to live there.

Epilogue

Although the events related to the disembodied spirit occurred more than forty years ago, they remain quite vivid in my mind (encounters with disembodied spirits are not easily forgotten). A second part of the tale was a condensation of decades of reflection which actually had this event as its root cause. Lessons learned in the mind often require years to sift down and settle in the soul. Perhaps this is why Jesus used agricultural models when speaking of "the Kingdom." The learning of the soul involves more than mere knowledge or understanding. It is more of a change in one's being. It involves a shift in one's perspective – a rearrangement of deep-seated values and premises. The end result is that whatever changes in behavior may occur are not the result of a change of intentional thinking, but the natural consequence of a new tree bearing new fruit. This, then, is my tale of relearning the balance between the mind, heart and soul in this spiritual journey which is the purpose of this life-on-earth. It also is a tale of an ongoing lover's quarrel I have with the Church. As a student of church history I have observed the Church at its best and its worst, and believe it has strayed off track along the way.

I believe some of the well-accepted doctrines are actually detrimental to spiritual health. They deal with fear, reward and punishment. None of these dynamics are conducive to freeing us from self-concern so we are free to act from love-of-God. Some of the teachings generate unnecessary guilt, shame and low self-image, which restrict our ability to venture forth with confidence into the world, stretch our boundaries and risk creating ideas and projects that could be new and worthy. We are made in the image of God, which by definition entails our being creative.

I have shared the story of the disembodied spirit with various people over the years. Some find it impossible to believe, and spend time trying to find a logical explanation. I well understand that reaction for, as the reader has learned, I spent much time doing the same . . . and I was in the midst of it. Others have found it easy to believe. Their own experience has led them to accept such things.

I refrained from writing this for many years for a variety of reasons. Primarily, I had promised the family involved that I would not reveal their names or situation. I believe that the passage of more than four decades has erased the necessity for that. I made a few false starts over the years. The first was halted abruptly when my computer crashed and destroyed the testing equipment of the repair shop. While waiting for the repair I used a substitute computer, which also crashed. While not being a superstitious sort, the remembrance of the events connected with the spirit were fresh enough in my mind to cause me to direct my attentions elsewhere.

Recently, my involvement with teaching and writing about spiritual growth reawakened the *poltergeist* episode. I realized anew the significance of the event for those who are willing to delve beneath the mere eeriness of the tale. As I wrote in my earlier book, *Can You Make the Buttons Even?*, "We are spiritual beings who are presently undergoing a physical existence." Earth is not our primary dwelling place. It is but a single, brief stopping place on a never-ending journey through eternity.

With this understanding, the story fell in place rather quickly. I had only to reach into my memory bank and draw out the details. I created the carpool conversations from a myriad of similar discussions I have had over the years. I did stay true to the general character of the participants, however, and the affection I felt for each. This time it was typed with no crashed computers and no concern that the curious might descend upon the family which hosted the spirit.

BEHIND THE STORY

The God Makers portion of this tale was a life-time in the making. I was on that path even before I entered the ministry. However it required years of observations and study to arrive at the point where Dick was with the carpool friends. Throughout the many years of my ministry I witnessed far too many clergy behave as though they had some special connection with Deity. Quite frankly I began in that mode. I assumed my special calling and seminary education gave me an edge. However, I quickly encountered far too many parishioners who obviously were much further along life's spiritual path than I. They possessed a wisdom born of experience that I still was seeking to discover. In every parish I have served I have found those who were more caring than I, more understanding than I, more deeply embedded in prayer than I, more likely to acknowledge their weaknesses than I . . . In short, they were more spiritually mature than I. Eventually, I realized the call to preach is simply that: *A call to preach.* It is no guarantee of a special understanding of Deity, or special mystical relationship which guarantees better response to prayers.

The call to preach, or proclaim, the Gospel should culminate in one receiving the training to understand the development and interpretation of Scripture and creeds. The preacher then utilizes these tools to share his/her personal journey in such a way that those who hear may be enabled to understand and shape their own journeys.

The preacher does this by sharing accounts from his or her journey and the journeys of others *they know to be true:* The struggles, failures and successes – and the insights gained along the way. Their calling never should be thought of as a license to proclaim *absolute truths*.

Early in my seminary career I noticed the extraordinary variety of images of Deity presented by highly educated, experienced clergy. Many seemed to be shaped more by the individual's political leanings than by Scripture. Most images appeared to be more reflective of the individual's personality than shaped by creeds. The more loving the professor, the more loving the deity. The more militant the professor, the more militant the deity. I soon began to think of Scripture as a combination record of past events and Rorschach test. To quote from Paul's letter to the Corinthians (I Corinthians 13:12):

> *Now we see in a mirror dimly, but then we shall see face to face. Now I know only in part; then I shall know fully, even as I have been fully known."*

When I began my doctoral studies I was appalled at the arrogance of those who formulated and defended the creeds. I also understood and was sympathetic to their plight. The church needed to refine its understanding of God, Jesus Christ, Holy Spirit, Sin and Salvation so that the message was not totally dissipated. What they failed to consider, however, was the extent to which their particular culture and personal experience shaped these understanding. For example, the prevailing philosophy of the Western Church was Stoicism which relied heavily upon certain assumptions about natural law. Add to this the fact that Roman culture revolved around the centrality of law coupled with the Jewish emphasis upon Law and you easily understand how the ideas of guilt, forgiveness, reward and punishment became decisive factors in shaping western theology. With the passage of time the concept of a relentlessly loving and forgiving parent deity, as revealed by Jesus, was sidetracked, and Western Christianity reverted to the legalism of the Pharisees, so distained by Jesus.

Meanwhile, the Eastern (Orthodox) Church, drawing more from Platonic thought asserted that "The Divine became human so that the human could become divine." They had no formal doctrine of atonement and did not see Christ's death as a sacrifice needed to pacify an angry, unforgiving deity. However, because of their world view and understanding of deity they required a redeemer who was eternal and fully divine. Their reasoning was simple: Anything that was created was capable of change; anything that changed eventually would decay and die. Ergo: Only that which was uncreated could bestow eternal life on mortals.

Ironically, today we are more likely to believe that only those persons who are capable of change can survive. We view life as a process, not as a static reality.

The great division which began in the second century and culminated in the 4th century was a dispute about a single Greek letter: *iota*. The insertion of this letter into a key word changed the description of Jesus as "similar to God" rather than "the same as God." In a time when there was wide-spread lawlessness, devastating wars, and much poverty, the church dissipated its resources bickering over an issue that actually was beyond anyone's capability to define. This, incidentally, resulted in the formulation of the Nicene Creed's phrase, "Begotten not made, being of one substance with the Father . . . .." There are those who believe this should be a required statement of belief for church membership today, although as a practical matter, this phase has no meaning in the existing world view . . . unless one wishes to suggest that God has a specific DNA.

To find support for this idea of Jesus being eternal and therefore capable of bestowing salvation, some theologian stumbled across the 1st century letter of Bishop Polycarp's which contained this phrase: "The medicine of our immortality." Since Polycarp was an early martyr his words carried special authority. As one surveyed Scripture the meaning seemed quite clear: At the institution of the Lord's Supper Jesus had stated that the bread was his body and the wine was his blood. The prevailing world view had no comprehension of atomic structure, or genetic material. That which we now call "essence" was dubbed "substance," and believed to inform matter of its nature. With a bit of creative theologizing it was decided that in the celebration of the Lord's Supper, the underlying "substance" of the bread and wine were transformed into the actual substance of Christ. If one ingested them in faithfulness their nature would be transformed over time to be the same as that of Christ – thus eternal. This became the doctrine known as "transubstantiation."

Please note that this was not thought to be magical hocus pocus. The ritual required that the participant be a true and faithful follower of Jesus Christ for the transformation to occur. This participation in the

Eucharist therefore might be considered to be "an outward and visible sign of an inward and spiritual grace."

During the time of the Reformation this doctrine created far more confusion and divisiveness than the earlier church ever considered possible. Luther split with Zwingli because he professed "consubstantiation" while Zwingli thought of the Last Supper as a moment in which the participant was transported in time to the first upper room, sharing in the meal with Christ Each one was so certain that he was correct – and the other wrong – that they could not cooperate in their attempt to reform the church.

The Church of the Inquisition was as guilty of mind control as the Soviet Union in the last half of the 20th century. In order to maintain the authority of Scripture they believed it necessary to suppress any idea which opposed any subject contained therein. The treatment of Galileo over his theory of "the movement of the Earth" by Pope Urban VIII was a travesty. However, try as it might, the church could not hold back the tide of history. The Enlightenment erupted shortly after, and science became free of the shackles the Church had placed upon it for centuries. It is sad that there are those today who would try to duplicate the failure of the medieval Church.

It is my experience that many weekly pew sitters do not agree with the message coming from the pulpit. They may not voice their disagreements for fear of ostracism. Still their minds are not enlightened, their lives are not guided, and their souls are not comforted by the weekly homily. They participate for a variety of reasons, *e.g.* habit, friendships, worthy activities. In the present culture, an increasing number of people no longer feel obligated to attend worship or even hold church membership. Their emphasis is more on spirituality than upon religion. In this regard I have noted an increasing number of books by secular (non-religious) writers in the spirituality section of local book dealers.

At this point I hasten to add that I also have observed great spiritual vitality within many congregations. Sometimes this is aided by the clergy. Sometimes it is in spite of clergy involvement, interference, or non-involvement. I am convinced that spiritual growth is quite possible within the framework of organized religion. It just is not inherent, always available, nor exclusively confined to established churches.

Finally, dear reader, if you have stayed with me this far, I have two more thoughts for your consideration:

1st. Words do not convey meaning to the reader or listener so much as they elicit meanings from the reader or listener. Words are abstractions we use to express a reality of thought, action or experience that transcends the ability of mere words to fully express it. Just as a series of photos – no matter how clear and detailed – cannot convey the wonder of experiencing a Grand Canyon, for instance, so words always must fall short of fully conveying a thought.

Because each of us has our own unique set of life experiences we each also have our own unique definitions of many key words. Some words carry strong emotional meaning for some but remain quite neutral for others. The simple term, *tree* generates very different images in people's minds, depending upon their locale and topography. *Cold* means one thing to Aleutians and another to Hawaiians. *Hunger* invokes very different images and emotional responses to a third world child than it does to a child of the American suburbs. Martin Luther had trouble saying "Our Father" simply because his experience of a father was quite unpleasant. "*A long time*" means one thing to a child and another to a senior citizen. The list is endless. This is one reason members of a group may hear the same sermon or speech and walk away with different understandings of what was said. It is for this reason that people should at least attempt to clarify key terms before entering into difficult and complex discussions.

2nd: We tend to express subjective experience as an objective fact. We do this as a matter of course in every day interchanges. A few examples:

"That was a great dinner!"   (I enjoyed it immensely)
"What a beautiful painting!"   (It appeals to me.)
"Bill is a great guy!"   (I like Bill a lot.)
"The speech was brilliant." (I agree with everything said)

Someone with different tastes and perspectives might give entirely different adjectives to the same experiences. They also would be stated as fact, and might debate with each side insisting that their appraisal is correct, rather than understanding and acknowledging the subjectivity involved.

If we study the creeds carefully, realizing that Scripture properly proclaims that no one but the Son has seen the Father, we must realize and acknowledge that all statements about the nature of Deity are necessarily *subjective experiences – not objective realities.* There are many varied doctrines of Jesus of Nazareth as Christ

(Anointed One) of God, Spirit-filled Messiah, Son of God, Word Incarnate, God Incarnate, or Son of Man. Most of these are mutually exclusive doctrines. One cannot be both Son of God and God Incarnate at the same time, for example. Yet most Christians use these terms interchangeably because – underlying each term is *the sincere belief that in Jesus of Nazareth they have experienced both the human and the divine.*

In the final analysis Jesus said we are judged by the quality of fruit produced by our lives. We are not judged by the specific type of fruit (or by the fertilizer spread upon us). I have come to believe that Jesus was not so concerned with our learning a specific systematic process, but with us finding a working relationship with the One he called Father. Each of us is responsible for shaping the quality of our own life. We would do well to be about the task of blending *our* unique life experiences with *our* informed understandings to shape *our* personal relationship with *our* God and the world in which we live. As we do this we will know *through our own experience* the Presence of the Creator of the Universe working in and through our lives.

No two people begin in the same place. No two journeys are identical. Paul said it well (Ephesians 2:12-13):

> *You must work out your own salvation in*
> *fear and in trembling for it is*
> *God who works in you to will and to act*
> *according to his good purpose."*

LaVergne, TN USA
11 August 2010
192903LV00001B/18/P